U BUDDHA

108 Mindfulness Lessons
for Surviving Test Stress, Freshman 15, Friend Drama,
Insane Roommates, Awkward Dates, Late Nights,
Morning Lectures ... and Other College Challenges

VICTOR M. PARACHIN

Ulysses Press

Published in the United States by:
Ulysses Press
P.O. Box 3440
Berkeley, CA 94703
www.ulyssespress.com

ISBN13: 978-1-61243-594-7
Library of Congress Control Number: 2016934487

Printed in the Canada by Marquis Book Printing

10 9 8 7 6 5 4 3 2 1

Acquisitions Editor: Kelly Reed
Managing Editor: Claire Chun
Project editor: Serena Lynn
Editor: Renee Rutledge
Proofreader: Lauren Harrison
Front cover and interior design: what!design @ whatweb.com
Cover artwork: lotus © Zorana Matijasevic/shutterstock.com; monk © 1507kot/shutterstock.com; backround pattern © Transia Design

Distributed by Publishers Group West

NOTE TO READERS: This book is independently authored and published and no sponsorship or endorsement of this book by, and no affiliation with, any trademarked brands or other products mentioned within is claimed or suggested. All trademarks that appear in ingredient lists and elsewhere in this book belong to their respective owners and are used here for informational purposes only. The authors and publishers encourage readers to patronize the quality brands mentioned in this book.

CONTENTS

INTRODUCTION

One recent survey discovered that as many as eight out of ten college students said they frequently experienced stress in their lives. That was an increase of more than 20 percent from surveys done five years earlier.

The fact is that college life can be highly stressful and is not the idyllic experience often portrayed in movies and books. As a college student, some of the most common stresses you face are:

❀ the application process

❀ grade competition

❀ performance anxiety

❀ romantic relationships

❀ establishing new friendships

❀ making career choices

❀ roommate issues

❀ loneliness

* working a part-time job while in school

* managing finances

As college stress increases and builds pressure, you need to find ways to manage the emotional strain and mental burden. More than 2,600 years ago, the Buddha taught a path for dealing with stress, reducing suffering and deepening happiness. The tools and concepts he offered then continue to be highly effective, user-friendly, readily accessible and easily applicable for college life today.

In this book, *Buddha U*, there are 108 Buddhist teachings that you can utilize to survive test stress, the freshman 15, friend drama, insane roommates, awkward dates, late nights, morning lectures and other college challenges. For Buddhism, 108 is a symbolic number with a variety of interpretations. One interpretation is that of completeness. Thus, in Japan, many Buddhist temples will chime a bell 108 times to signify the completion of one year while welcoming a new one. As you go through your college year, let yourself be guided by these 108 mindful lessons. As you put them into practice, you will find yourself ending one academic year with immense satisfaction and anticipating the new one with great enthusiasm.

—Victor M. Parachin

DAY 1

FORGET THE FRIEND DRAMA

*When you keep bad company, your activities of hearing,
thinking and meditating decline, and they make you
lose your love and compassion. Give up bad friends.*

~Gyalsay Togme Sangpo

Bad friends don't have horns. Good friends don't have halos.
It isn't possible to tell a good friend from a bad friend merely
by appearances. Yet college is a place where new and often
lifelong relationships are made. Thus, it's important that the
people closest to you are good friends. The Buddha consistently
stressed the vital importance of cultivating positive, healthy
friendships, saying, "An insincere and bad friend is more to be
feared that a wild beast. A wild beast may wound your body but a
bad friend will wound your mind."

Because one cannot identify a bad companion from a good
one by simple observation, Buddhism suggests choosing friends
based on these kinds of general characteristics and qualities:
A good friend is someone who is honest, ethical, has integrity,
exhibits a kind heart, speaks warmly and gently, and is humble
and good-natured. This kind of friend can help you evolve

ethically, morally, emotionally and spiritually. Even if this friend doesn't directly talk about ethics and morals, his or her example will influence you in those positive directions.

On the other hand, a bad friend is someone who leans toward negative, poisonous emotions or actions, such as anger, gossip, unkindness, being judgmental and cruelty. These traits will have an adverse effect upon you. By keeping company with this type of person, the virtues you have developed can be halted and even deteriorate and degenerate.

So, the advice of the thirteenth century Tibetan Buddhist teacher Gyalsay Togme Sangpo is sound: "Give up bad friends." Of course, doing so does not mean that you consider yourself superior to them or lack compassion for them. It is a simple recognition that their negative energy can become a hindrance to your own growth and development. Be courteous and civil toward them, but maintain healthy boundaries.

DAY **2**

SURVIVING TEST STRESS

Pain is inevitable. Misery is optional.

~Victor M. Parachin

Rising early one morning, Korean Zen Master Kyong Ho (1849–1912) and his disciple Man Gong were in a village begging for food. At the time, the two men were living alone in a small hermitage and were dependent upon kind villagers for their daily food. So, they had to gather rice and take it back to their hermitage. This day, the villagers were very generous, filling their large rice bag to the very top.

Because Man Gong was the student and Kyong Ho his teacher, tradition called for Man Gong to carry the heavy bag of rice most of the way home. With the bag on his back, Man Gong struggled to carry the bag and, with several miles left to walk, began to complain how heavy the bag was, how hard it was for him to keep up and how tired he was becoming.

As they passed through a tiny village, a young woman came out of a building carrying a water jug on her head. She was walking toward Kyong Ho and just as their paths were about to cross, Kyong Ho grabbed her and passionately kissed her on the lips. (His action was in keeping with the style of some Zen masters who often behaved erratically and outrageously in order to drive home a lesson.) Shocked, the woman's water jug fell to the ground, breaking. She ran back into the building, screaming hysterically.

Within a few seconds, her father, mother, aunts, uncles, brothers and sisters charged out of the building holding knives, clubs and sticks. Kyong Ho and Man Gong, still carrying the bag of rice, ran as fast as they could, barely remaining ahead of the angry mob. When they reached the edge of town, the villagers finally gave up.

As the two men stood there breathing heavily, Kyong Ho looked at Man Gong with a smile, asking: "So, was the bag of rice heavy as you ran?" Man Gong responded: "Heavy? I completely forgot I had it on my back as I ran to get away from the villagers." Then Kyong Ho made his point: "Aren't you luck to have me as your teacher? Before you had heavy on your mind, but now you have attained no-heavy."

Look closely at what happened to Man Gong. The bag of rice weighed the same when he was struggling to keep up with Kyong Ho and when he was running for his life from the villagers. The only thing that changed was his thinking. Rather than place his focus on how heavy the bag of rice was, his thought shifted to running and remaining ahead of his pursuers.

Man Gong offers an important lesson because there are times in life when we all carry a "bag of rice" on our shoulders. It can be the burden of loneliness, heartache, depression or disappointment. In life, pain is inevitable. Misery, however, is optional. A burden can become unbearable only when you allow yourself to wallow in self-pity, adding misery to the already-present pain. On the other hand, a burden can become quite manageable when you cease obsessing about it and shift your thoughts toward positive, constructive areas of your life.

Try moving from heavy on your mind to no-heavy. For instance, if you have a big final tomorrow, instead of being preoccupied about the possibility of getting a bad grade, refocus on the subject material.

DAY **3**

COLLEGE ISN'T A BEAUTY PAGEANT

Life is difficult.

~First Noble Truth of Buddhism

Think about stained glass windows, the type commonly found in churches. Though they are beautiful, it's worth noting that they are made from bits and pieces of broken glass.

Think about your own life. Consider the parts of you that have undergone an experience of being broken, perhaps a frustrating childhood, a difficult relationship, betrayal by someone close to you, being excluded by the "in" group, the death of a family member or good friend. Seemingly there can be no end to difficulties that come. That's why the Buddha declared as the first of four "noble" truths that life comes with difficulty or suffering.

Like the pieces of broken glass that create beautiful stained glass windows, the broken part of our lives can be taken and re-arranged or re-structured, creating something beautiful to behold. We should never permit our pain to be wasted but used for our growth and for the good of others. This was something noted by author physician Elizabeth Kubler Ross:

Beautiful people we have known are those who have known defeat, known suffering, known struggle, known loss, and have found their way out of the depths....
These persons have an appreciation, a sensitivity, and an understanding of life that fills them with compassion, gentleness, and a deep, loving concern. Beautiful people do not just happen.

Be one of those beautiful people on your campus.

DAY **4**

RETURN A LOST ID CARD

How people treat you is their karma. How you react is yours.

~Wayne W. Dyer

The word "karma" is a Sanskrit term. It literally means an act or an action. The essence of karma is simple: If an action taken is positive, there will be a positive result. If an action taken is negative, there will be a negative response.

We've all experienced the results of karma. If you're agitated, rude or disrespectful toward those around you, you nearly always receive the same in return from them. However, when you are patient, kind or accepting, those same qualities are nearly always returned to us from others.

The consequences of karma are either negative or positive. It's entirely up to you as to what kind of karma you create moment by moment and day by day. For example, when you decide to do yoga or exercise in general, the consequence will be better physical and emotional health. Conversely, when you decide not to exercise or watch your food consumption, then the consequence will be deteriorating physical and emotional health.

Furthermore, you can strengthen and energize your own good karma by responding rather than reacting to another person's offensive behavior. If someone shows you disrespect, you can respond with courtesy; if someone speaks rudely to you, you can respond with kindness; and, if someone is impatient and harsh with you, you can respond with patience and compassion.

Karma means you are not powerless. You have the power, the ability and the responsibility to make change happen! You have the ability to influence your life in ways that create and generate positive vibes.

DAY **5**

SURVIVING A BAD SEMESTER

*There is a reason you can learn from everything: you have
basic wisdom, basic intelligence and basic goodness.*

~Pema Chodron

Here's some common sense: as long as you're going to suffer,
then learn to suffer well! These are characteristics of people who
learn to practice "good" suffering:

- ❋ They learn from their suffering.
- ❋ They don't waste the pain but use it to help and enrich others.
- ❋ They allow suffering to make themselves better, not bitter.
- ❋ They turn inward, tapping into latent powers and resources.
- ❋ They believe in themselves and their ability to overcome.
- ❋ They view the future with optimism and hope.
- ❋ They demonstrate strong character and act out of their highest self.
- ❋ They ask for help when needed.

BUDDHA U

When you go through a tough time, bring to mind the wisdom of the Buddha: "No one saves us but ourselves. No one can and no one may. We must walk the path." Then tell yourself: "If it's going to be, then it's up to me!" Begin to practice good suffering.

DAY **6**

JOIN A CLUB

There are, strictly speaking, no enlightened people, there is only enlightened activity.

~-Shunryu Suzuki

One aspect of Buddhism that endlessly fascinates people is enlightenment. Yet, Zen master Shunryu Suzuki states that "there are no enlightened people, there is only enlightened activity."

So, what is enlightenment?

To understand, begin with what it is not. Enlightenment is not:

❀ being in a constant state of bliss

❀ having supernatural powers and insights

❀ receiving visions or hearing voices

Rather, enlightenment is:

❀ living with awareness

❀ acting mindfully

❀ expressing consistent compassion toward all beings

Any person, whether they are Buddhist, Christian, Muslim, Jewish, agnostic or atheist, who displays the attitude of non-

BUDDHA U

harming and nonviolence may rightly be described as living a life of enlightenment. So, when Suzuki says, "There are no enlightened people, there is only enlightened activity," he offers a profound and practical insight, namely, that enlightenment is not a state to arrive at, but a style of life to live out. This planet needs more people who engage in enlightened activity.

Are you one of them?

DAY **7**

HOLDING DOWN A PART-TIME JOB BETWEEN CLASSES

The most important things in life aren't things.

~Anthony J. D'Angelo

Here is a concise but profound spiritual teaching by Atisha (982–1054 CE), a Buddhist from India who taught extensively in Tibet. Whenever you lament your circumstances, such as the part-time job you wish you could skip, ponder Atisha's wisdom.

The greatest achievement is selflessness.

The greatest worth is self-mastery.

The greatest quality is seeking to serve others.

The greatest precept is continual awareness.

The greatest medicine is the emptiness of everything.

The greatest action is not conforming to the world's ways.

The greatest magic is transmuting the passions.

The greatest generosity is non-attachment.

The greatest goodness is a peaceful mind.

The greatest patience is humility.

The greatest effort is not concerned with results.

The greatest meditation is a mind that lets go.

The greatest wisdom is seeing through appearances.

DAY **8**

WHEN YOUR PROFESSOR HAS IT IN FOR YOU

*That the birds of worry and care fly over your
head, this you cannot change, but that they build
nests in your hair, this you can prevent.*

~Buddhist Proverb

The next time troubles come your way and worries begin to chip away at you, take a deep breath and think it all through. Basically, that's the wisdom offered by Shantideva, an eighth century Buddhist spiritual master. Here's how he put it:

"A difficult situation can be handled in two ways: We can either do something to change it, or we can face it.

If we can do something, then why worry and get upset over it—just change it!

If there is nothing we can do, again, why worry and get upset over it? Things will not get better with anger and worry."

When facing a difficulty, ask yourself: "Can I change it?" If the answer is yes, then work toward making a change. If the answer is no, then just face it and drop the worry because worrying can't make it better, only worse.

The popular "Serenity Prayer" makes the same point:

God grant me the serenity
to accept the things I cannot change;
courage to change the things I can;
and wisdom to know the difference.

DAY **9**

WALK IN A PEACE RALLY

*If aggression is an innate impulse, so is gentleness and
the ability to go beyond our murderous instincts.*

~Georg Feuerstein

The Buddha was a fan of his contemporary spiritual teacher, a man named Mahavira, founder of the Jain religion. There are several recorded texts which indicate that the Buddha and the religion which bears his name were deeply influenced by Mahavira. One aspect of Buddhism impacted by Mahavira is his teaching about nonviolence. The Sanskrit term for this concept is *ahimsa*, which literally means "non-harming."

While we often think of this concept in terms of not killing, *ahimsa* includes goes far beyond that to teaching that the key to non-harming is attentive, careful vigilance. To ensure that this vigilance is cultivated, these nine practices are cited as vital:

1. Guarding one's speech

2. Guarding one's thoughts

3. Care in walking

4. Care in lifting and laying down things

5. Careful inspection of one's food and drink

6. Benevolence toward all beings

7. Delight in all beings

8. Compassion for all beings

9. Patience and understanding toward all those who are misguided in behavior

Take some time to go over these, understanding their meaning and assessing their place in your daily life.

DAY **10**

SHARE YOUR NOTES

*It is incumbent on all to stop hurting and harming others
and cultivate a boundless heart full of benevolence.*

~Piyadassi Thera

How would your life and the lives of those around you change if:

- ❀ you saw winners, not sinners
- ❀ you chose acceptance over judgment
- ❀ you cultivated constant gratitude rather than indifference
- ❀ you reached out rather than held back
- ❀ you did more giving and less receiving
- ❀ you focused on the positive and not on the toxic
- ❀ you listened more and spoke less
- ❀ you greeted hostility with hospitality
- ❀ you encouraged the discouraged
- ❀ you tried to turn sadness into gladness
- ❀ you smiled sincerely and boldly at everyone you saw
- ❀ you expanded love and enlarged mercy

BUDDHA U

❋ you lived with confidence and faith

❋ you expressed compassion to all human and animal
   beings

How different would things be if you and others acted and
lived out these patterns of life?

DAY 11

BE THE FRIENDLIEST FACE ON CAMPUS

All know the way; few actually walk it.

~Bodhidharma

Doing good should not be simply an ideal but a reality. It is something done immediately and in the present, moment by moment.

That's what poet William Blake had in mind when he wrote, "If one is to do good, it must be done in the minute particulars. General good is the plea of the hypocrite, the scoundrel, and the flatterer."

Most people want to do good, but they delay it. And good delayed is good denied. If this is a pattern in your life, change it immediately. Do good *and* do it now, today, this very moment as opportunity presents itself. Do good to your family, your friends, your roommate, your teachers, strangers, animals and birds, plants and herbs, the great trees of the forests.

Centuries ago, there was a famous Chinese Buddhist monk who meditated high up in a tree. His location was dangerous because one sleepy nod during meditation meant he could fall out of the tree, severely injuring or even killing himself. He came to be known as "Bird's Nest." As his reputation spread, people often came to him seeking advice about life. One day an important government official visited him and shouted up, "Bird's Nest, what is the best way to live?" The monk responded, "Do good. Never do bad." The official, expecting some deeper philosophy and wisdom, was very disappointed with this simple, straightforward advice and said, "Do good. Never do bad. Everyone knows that. There must be more." Bird's Nest told him, "Everyone knows that but very few people do that."

Be the person on your campus who knows the way *and* walks the way; the one whose ideals show up in the realities of daily life.

DAY 12

HOW TO ACE YOUR FINALS

*Our mind is a field in which every kind of
seed is sown—seeds of compassion, joy and
hope, seeds of sorrow, fear and difficulty.*

~Thich Nhat Hanh

Your mind is like a fertile plot of rich earth. Moment by moment and minute by minute, you are constantly seeding it. Test this view by thinking about your day yesterday. What seeds—feelings, emotions, qualities—did you permit to enter your awareness?

Were they seeds of fear, anxiety, pain, stress, anger, trouble, unease? Or were they seeds of hope, faith, love, joy, peace, kindness, goodness?

You must develop the skill of a master gardener and be intentional about which seeds will be planted. Be diligent in providing the proper "nutrients" for mind seeds to flourish and grow. Water what you want to grow!

You can do this even if you grew up in a family and culture where most expressions were negative, pessimistic and cynical. You can learn to think, speak and act differently. Just keep remembering that you have the power to shape your thoughts.

BUDDHA U

Starting right now, use these types of positive, empowering statements to nourish your mind and make you feel more capable, confident and courageous:

- ❀ I am a positive person who views people and life optimistically.

- ❀ I like myself and feel good about who I am, how I look and how I act.

- ❀ I can accomplish anything I put my mind to.

- ❀ I am talented and therefore willing to assume risks.

- ❀ I feel good, strong, healthy and sound in body, mind and spirit.

- ❀ I am loving, compassionate and sensitive toward everyone I encounter.

- ❀ I face problems courageously, identifying the positive potential present.

- ❀ I love life and begin each day with enthusiasm and hope.

DAY **13**

SUPPORT YOUR PEERS

The potential of the average person is like a huge ocean unsailed, a new continent unexplored, a world of possibilities waiting to be released and channeled toward some great good.

~Brian Tracy

Swami Sivananda was a medical doctor who left his medical practice to become a Hindu spiritual teacher. As more and more people began seeking out his teachings, he established an ashram near Rishikesh. There, people from all over India would go to see him. This included many artists, writers and musicians who would visit the ashram, offering their talents and services.

One time, a young man came to a public event and said to the Swami, "I am a flute player and would like to perform for you." Swami Sivananda said, "Good. Let us listen to you." The entire community was present as the young man began playing his flute. It became apparent almost immediately that he was a beginner. His flute playing was very poor and he sounded terrible. When he finished the piece of music, Swami Sivananda looked at him and said in all seriousness, "Wonderful! Wonderful! I award you the title of master flutist." When the young man left, Swami

Sivananda's students questioned him, "How could you say that? Why did you give him a title? It will make compliments and titles meaningless."

Swami Sivananda disregarded the comments and criticisms. Almost one year later, the young man returned to an event at the ashram and said, "Swami Sivananda, I want to thank you for giving me the title of master flutist last year. I would like to play for you again." The Swami said, "Please do so."

This time, his music was flawless and enthralling, and moved those who heard him play.

Swami Sivananda demonstrates the power all of us have to unleash someone's potential. This is easy to do by encouraging them, taking them seriously, and conveying the fact that you believe in them. How many talented people never evolved simply because they had no one to cheer them on at a pivotal moment in their lives?

DAY **14**

LOOK INTO STUDYING ABROAD

*Look and you will find it—what is
unsought will go undetected.*

~Sophocles

A young college woman attended a lecture by Carl Jung, the Swiss psychiatrist and founder of what has come to be called Jungian psychology. Following his lecture she had an opportunity to ask him, "Could you tell me the shortest path to my life's goal or purpose?" Without hesitation, Jung replied, "The detour!"

Think about his answer. First, a detour is a deviation from a path. Second, rather than view the detour as an inconvenience or disruption, Jung implies that detours deserve a serious second and positive look; that, in fact, the new path we are forced onto may be the very place where our highest good and our highest goals are realized.

The story of the Buddha and Buddhism can be summed up as the result of his life detour. His story is that of a person born into great wealth, a royal family in India. His path was to continue the royal line and follow in the footsteps of his father. However, he came across a detour when he observed the deep suffering of people. Intuitively, he knew that his place in life would be that of a spiritual teacher offering guidance and wisdom for dealing with life's problems and potentials. Thus, he renounced his heritage and took the detour.

Like the Buddha, you should permit a detour to become your awakening. This happened recently to a friend who, in midlife, went into depression. In addition, he was diagnosed with high blood pressure. Rather than simply take medication for both conditions, he took inventory of his life, making some changes. He began to bike for 45 minutes daily and started attending a weekly meditation group. As a result, his blood pressure lowered and his depression lifted.

DAY **15**

TURN AWAY FROM DORM ROOM GOSSIP

Right speech is endeared with the four characteristics of being apt and fitting, fair, endearing and truthful.

~Buddha

Too often, people hear words that injure. Painfully absent are words that inspire. That's why the Buddha emphasized the importance of right speech.

Today, commit yourself to spreading words such as these, all of which will encourage and lift up the people you encounter across your campus:

- ❀ I feel honored to know you.

- ❀ I love your smile.

- ❀ Please forgive me.

- ❀ You are fabulous.

- ❀ Let me help.

- ❀ You're such a kind person.

- ❀ It's always good to see you.

❀ You go first.

❀ You make me happy and proud.

❀ I've missed you.

❀ You inspire me.

❀ I'm so glad you are my friend.

❀ I believe in you and support you.

❀ You have a beautiful smile.

❀ You are someone to be celebrated.

❀ I love you.

DAY **16**

WHEN YOU'RE NOT INVITED TO THE PARTY

Let no one speak harshly to another. Angry
words bring troubles and blows in return.

~Dhammapada

Whenever someone mistreats you or when there is a personal setback, disappointment or failure, you can react in of these ways:

Blow up. This takes the form of anger and resentment. This action also includes blaming others or conditions. It avoids assessing responsibility.

Cover up. Here a person chooses to hide from his or her failure. The motive behind covering up is to protect one's image.

Back up. We've all seen people who rush into retreat. "I'll never try that again" is their attitude. This person is unwilling to learn from mistakes and setbacks.

Give up. One of the worst things anyone can do is throw up their hands and quit. Doing this is an indication that a person is lacking in persistence, perseverance and patience.

Step up. This person is able to rise and meet the challenge honestly, boldly and courageously. It requires the ability to override feelings of fear, anger and frustration.

The first four are generally the result of reacting emotionally and thoughtlessly. The last one, and the best one, comes from responding with skill, wisdom and maturity.

What's your emotional style when things don't go your way?

DAY **17**

WHEN YOU'RE HAVING
TROUBLE SLEEPING

Death is not to be feared by one who has lived wisely.

~Buddha

A short news story reported that a couple had developed a new board game called Funeral Director: A Race to Your Final Resting Place. It is designed to help people deal with their own mortality by taking the fear out of death. The game has players move tiny coffins around the board and, in the process, make arrangement for their funerals. Players even get to choose how they die:

- ❀ die laughing
- ❀ die of boredom
- ❀ die of a broken heart
- ❀ die of fright

They also get to decide what kind of funeral they want, with choices ranging from cremation, burial at sea, something environmentally sound or burial on the family farm.

Time will tell if the game will be popular.

However, the developers probably don't know that they've developed a game that could easily be described as a Buddhist tool for thinking about death. Buddhists are fond of placing their focus on death. It is common for Tibetan Buddhist monks to spend their morning meditation by focusing and thinking about death. The reason is simple: the goal of Buddhism is to improve life and the best way to improve life now is by thinking about and realizing that we will all die.

In the West, we do something similar any time we ask ourselves, "What should I do with my life?" Behind that question is the realization that our time here is brief and that we should spend our lives wisely. No one on his or her death bed ever says "I wish I had worked more" or "I wish I had a bigger house" or "I wish I had a luxury car," etc.

Pondering death can help us know more clearly what to do with our time here. As you think about your life, ask yourself, "What is the best use of my life?" Listen carefully for the answer.

DAY **18**

CHOOSING YOUR MAJOR

*If you follow your bliss, you put yourself on a kind of
track that has been there all the while, waiting for you.*

~Joseph Campbell

Today, ask yourself this question: "Am I following my *calling* or am I following my *conditioning*?" Generally, following a calling leaves one feeling fulfilled, while following conditioning leaves one feeling dissatisfied with life. A calling is something felt inwardly. Conditioning comes outwardly, usually in the form of fitting into expectations others have for us.

One man tells of becoming a successful corporate lawyer. Though he enjoyed being part of a prestigious profession which came with a luxurious income, he did not feel fulfilled. Reflecting on his life, he realized he was following conditioning and not his calling. Why was this the case? Because his father was a lawyer, his brother was a lawyer, his mother was a lawyer and his aunt was a lawyer. Basically, he studied and trained to enter a family business. This path was both practical and sensible yet, as a lawyer, he found himself both unhappy and unfulfilled. Every weekday, he had to persuade himself to get up and practice law.

Finally, he began to explore options for himself. Concluding that another path would bring him greater fulfillment, he left the lucrative practice of law to become a social worker. Today, he looks forward to each day, bringing passion and enthusiasm to his work.

Calling or conditioning? Which path are you following?

DAY **19**

GROWING YOUR FRIEND CIRCLE

The idea that some lives matter less is the
root of all that's wrong with the world.

~Paul Farmer

Many generations ago in ancient India, a Buddhist master was teaching outdoors before a large group. As he taught, a dog nearby began barking louder and louder. Evidently it annoyed one man in the audience, who picked up a rock and threw it, hitting the dog on the left side. At that very moment, the Buddhist master fell to the ground, crying out in pain and holding his left side. Later in the evening, his disciples further inspected his rib area, finding a large, dark bruise there. Evidently, the dog's pain at being struck by a rock became the master's pain as well.

Though that story may be metaphorical, what is true is that Buddhism teaches compassion to all beings. On that teaching, the Buddha is alone among the great founders of religions. Where the others all teach kindness, generosity and compassion to other human beings, the Buddha differs in that he stressed the importance of extending those virtuous acts to animals, birds, insects, worms, crickets, mosquitoes and more. The Buddha taught and encouraged us to have noble, tender hearts toward *all* sentient beings. The truth is that they, like humans, want the same thing: to be happy and to not suffer.

Remember to extend your innate compassion to them. Remind your family, friends and coworkers the importance of doing that as well. Everyone, everywhere should work at enlarging their compassion circle to include all beings, not just human beings.

DAY **20**

STUDYING AT A LOUD CAFE

Each of us literally chooses, by his way of attending to things, what sort of universe he shall appear to himself to inhabit.

~William James

A man was jogging through the foothills of Southern California when he suddenly froze in place. In the dim light of early morning, he saw a rattlesnake lying in the sun just a few feet ahead. Slowly and carefully, he made his way around with his heart beating rapidly and his eyes widened. As he got a little closer, he realized it wasn't a snake, but a piece of thick rope.

With a smile on his face and relief in his heart, he began to step toward it and over it when he glanced down again, discovering that it was a money belt that had slipped from someone hiking through the mountains. This time, he gasped in awe at what he found.

That story, of course, has a readily obvious lesson: perception becomes reality. However, less obvious is this lesson: how many times in any given day does our perception lead us to an erroneous conclusion? For example, the clerk we experience as rude may simply be stressed out because her child struggles with cancer. Or, the "impatient" customer service representative who rushed us off the phone may have done that because he works for a firm which pressures their employees to end customer calls as quickly as possible. Or, the student who appears to snub us may simply be upset because of an argument with a boyfriend or girlfriend.

The fact is that our perceptions are constantly filtered through our own thoughts, feelings and emotions. It is a worthy reminder to be aware of your perceptions and conclusions. We are always wise when we soften judgment and allow compassion to shape our perceptions.

DAY **21**

FOCUS ON THE CLASS YOU ACED

When presented with disquieting thoughts or feelings, cultivate an opposite elevated attitude.

~Patanjali, Yoga Sutra II:33

Think about disquieting thoughts for a moment. A quick list could include anger, jealousy, fear, discouragement, depression, hopelessness, anxiety, powerlessness and more. In fact, psychologists say that we humans have a wide range of emotions, with some lists containing 1,000 different human feelings and emotions.

Ancient sages knew this truth about us and they also knew that, since there is such a wide variety of emotions, we could replace one thought or feeling for another thought or feeling. Patanjali is one such ancient sage who advised: "When presented with disquieting thoughts or feelings, cultivate an opposite *elevated* attitude."

When he says "elevated," he is saying replace one negative thought or emotion with a positive one. This is not difficult to do. It simply requires intention and mindfulness. For example:

When feeling anxious, replace it with trust;

When feeling hopeless, replace it with hope;

When feeling frightened, replace it with courage;

When feeling discouraged, replace it with confidence;

When feeling weak, replace it with strength.

When feeling powerless, replace it with anticipation.

It can be lifesaving to remember that what you experience begins in the mind. Poet John Milton expressed it this way: "The mind can make a heaven out of hell or hell out of heaven." So, if and when you are feeling sad, depressed or even hopeless, remember to cultivate an opposite elevated attitude.

DAY 22

GETTING ALONG WITH YOUR COLLEGE ROOMMATE

Truth is one but sages call it by many names.

~Rig Veda

Today, read and reflect on this provocative observation from Swami Satchidananda: More people have died in the name of God and religions than in all the wars and natural calamities. But the real purpose of any religion is to educate us about our spiritual unity. It is time for us to recognize that there is one truth and many approaches. The basic cause of all the world problems is the lack of understanding of our spiritual unity. The need of the hour is to know, respect, love one another and to live as one global family.

Just think what kind of change could take place in any community—including your campus community—if a critical mass of people would passionately embrace the reality that "truth is one."

This would mean dropping all religious divisions and distinctions.

This would mean no longer seeing Protestants and Catholics, Jews and Muslims, saved and unsaved.

This would mean understanding that truth is like a mountain with many paths leading to the top.

This would mean knowing that all people want the same thing: to be happy and not to suffer.

So, today in your community, live out Swami Satchidananda's call "to know, respect, love one another and to live as one global family."

DAY **23**

HOLDING THE CAFETERIA DOOR OPEN

As long as space endures and sentient
beings remain, may I remain and dispel
the miseries of the world.

~Shantideva

What's wrong with these two incidents:

First, a teenage boy driving carelessly through a neighborhood rides up a curb and strikes a mailbox. Residents see what has happened and come out threatening to beat the young man for the damage he has caused. Sometime later, in the same neighborhood, a teenage girl driving carelessly through the neighborhood rides up a curb and strikes a mailbox. This time, residents come out and ask kindly, "Are you all right?"

Second, after a woman is left paralyzed from a stroke, her daughter begins to care for her—feeding her, turning her over, helping to change her clothing, etc. She begins to find the care unpleasant and burdensome. At the same time, she tends kindly and compassionately to her baby, who also needs 24/7 care.

What's wrong with these two incidents is this: care, kindness and compassion are given out discriminatingly. A baby is worthy of care, but an elderly woman who needs similar care becomes the source of resentment. A teen girl in an auto accident becomes the source of compassion, but the teen boy is the brunt of anger.

What really needs to happen is a shift of perception. We all simply need to see people who need help and promptly offer to be of assistance. The philosophy of the Indian Buddhist sage Shantideva is one which all should adopt. Make an effort to dispel misery consistently, comprehensively and without making exceptions.

DAY **24**

WHEN YOUR BEST FRIEND'S BAE IS A JERK

Appear as someone's helper or teacher only when they are open and ready for growth. Recognize when you can best be the teacher that another person is seeking.

~Victor M. Parachin

An ancient Eastern story tells of a bitterly cold winter day overcast with clouds that blocked the warmth of the sun. A group of monkeys sat in a forest tree clinging to bunches of red berries, believing they were fiery, warm, red coals.

In the same tree lived a sparrow warmly huddled in her nest. Seeing the folly of the monkeys, the sparrow was moved with compassion to help them. The sparrow approached them gently, saying, "Friends, you can't get warm just by holding those red berries. Let me show you how to build a nest like mine and then you can live comfortably when it's cold."

Rather than respond with appreciation, the monkeys became angry, shouting back, "How dare you criticize us. Mind your own business! Who are you to tell us how to live?" Then, in a moment of rage at the sparrow for embarrassing them, they pounced on its nest, tearing it apart.

Here's the moral of that story: Though you may see another person in a difficult situation and you feel you can help, it may be better to hold back if the person is insecure, prone to anger or not yet ready to receive help. Don't teach those who have minds like monkeys.

DAY **25**

OVERCOMING PERFORMANCE ANXIETY

However small a spark may be, it can burn down a haystack as big as a mountain.

~Buddha

A girl, curious about yoga, asked her teacher how many yoga poses there were. He answered "approximately 84,000," which is what the yoga tradition teaches. Immediately, the little girl declared, "I want to learn them all." Gently, he said, "No, no, learn them one by one."

There is a great deal of wisdom in that simple story. To make big changes, we need to set small goals. Think of a small bird which needs to build a large nest in order to hold and shelter three or four babies. The bird will begin by flying off, seeking one twig and bringing it back to the tree branch. Then it goes and finds another twig or piece of string, returning to the branch again. This process is repeated, one by one, and after some time, there is a sturdy, sheltering nest ready.

To make big changes, set small goals:

If you want to run a marathon, learn to run one mile;

If you want to become a medical doctor, take a science course at community college;

If you want to find a new job, begin by preparing a resume;

If you want to_____ (fill in the blank), set this small goal_____(fill in the blank again).

DAY **26**

CULTIVATE THE LIVE/ STUDY BALANCE

Rise to the challenge of maintaining mental balance during the storms of life.

~Victor M. Parachin

Often when we receive unwelcome and unexpected news, we have an amazing tendency to freak out and panic. Recognizing this, Buddhism teaches us and reminds us to remain balanced, unmoving and with an unflappable mind. This is the meaning of the popular saying, "Keep your cool," when presented with an unpleasant situation.

An inspiring example of this mindset comes from Thich Nhat Hanh. Some time ago, fire inspectors came to Plum Village, his monastic center in the countryside of France. They said it needed to be closed because it wasn't up to code and was completely unsafe for residents. The estimate for bringing it up to code was nearly $2 million. The leaders at Plum Village were not only panic-stricken but heartbroken upon hearing the word "close."

Thich Nhat Hanh was visibly unaffected, telling those around him, "If we have to close, we can close. We don't need to run after $2 million." He recommended looking more closely and carefully at their situation. As it turned out, only $500,000 was needed to bring the property up to code, an amount which reasonable and reachable.

When a serious situation emerges in your personal or professional life, override the first instinct to panic and react. Instead, learn to remain calm and cool under the pressure. Some ways to cultivate a cool mind include:

⚜ Slowing down and taking time to absorb and understand what is going on.

⚜ Remaining less emotional and more rational about the situation.

⚜ Staying hopeful and positive, working for the best possible outcome.

⚜ Identifying good people who could provide emotional support and help you manage the crisis.

By functioning this way, you can overcome the crisis, remaining calm and focused when college life becomes a pressure cooker.

DAY **27**

EXPLORE OFF-CAMPUS SIGHTS

Set me, O Earth, amidst the nourishing strength that emanates from your body.

~Atharva Veda Book XII

The Buddha and his contemporaries spent a great deal of their time outdoors. They meditated, taught, ate and rested outside, in nature. To this day, all over Asia people spend a great deal of their time outside believing that doing so promotes health and happiness. The Japanese have a custom called "shinrin-yoku" or forest bathing. This is simply a walk through a forest absorbing the scenery, listening to nature sounds and inhaling the scent of trees.

Now, science backs up their tradition, stating that forest bathing offers a health benefit. Researchers have discovered that exposure to trees and plants in a forest boosts immune function, increases cancer-battling proteins, lowers pulse rate, drops blood pressure and decreases stress levels, helping students feel greater well-being and do better in school. The benefit comes from phytoncides (wood essential oils), which trees and plants in

BUDDHA U

a forest emit to protect themselves from insects and disease. It is believed that they confer disease protection to humans as well.

Take advantage of their wisdom by thinking of activities you do indoors that could be done outdoors as well. Some suggestions: eating, exercising, reading, meditating, socializing, etc.

DAY **28**

BAD DATES HAPPEN

In order to properly understand the big picture,
everyone should fear becoming mentally clouded
and obsessed with one small section of truth.

~Xunzi

One day a traveler walking along a road came across three stonecutters working in a quarry. Each was busy cutting a block of stone. Curious about their activity, he asked the first stonecutter what he was doing.

"I am cutting a stone!"

Because the answer obviously wasn't helpful, the traveler turned to the second stonecutter and asked him what he was doing.

"I am cutting this block of stone to make sure that it's square, and its dimensions are uniform, so that it will fit exactly in its place in a wall."

While that was a little more informative, the traveler still didn't know what they were working on so he turned to the third stonecutter, who seemed to be the happiest of the three. When asked what he was doing the man replied:

"I am building a cathedral."

Consider the first two stonecutters. The first man had an extremely limited perspective: he was just cutting a rock. The second man's perspective was a little broader, taking into understanding that his work required him to cut carefully.

Now, consider closely the third man, who is set apart from the other two by his big-picture perspective:

❀ He not only knew how to cut and where to place the stones, but he knew *why* he was doing it;

❀ He saw the end result, not just a rubble of stone being cut into shapes;

❀ He knew that his work had significance beyond the daily cutting and chipping;

❀ Because of his vision, he found dignity and meaning in his work.

Each day, be like the third stonecutter and train yourself to see the bigger picture of your life. When that is done you will not become bogged down and frustrated by what is small, petty, shallow and insignificant.

DAY **29**

MARILYN MONROE'S BUDDHIST WISDOM

Buddha's nature is within every person. It reveals itself as good thoughts, good actions and wisdom.

~Victor M. Parachin

Though the actress Marilyn Monroe was presented by Hollywood studios as a Hollywood sex symbol, she also exhibited a Buddhist nature characterized by insight and wisdom. Here are some statements of hers that match the Buddhist view:

Marilyn: Women who seek to be equal with men lack ambition.

The Buddhist view: Tap into your potential and be all that you can be. You are better, larger and greater than you believe.

Marilyn: I believe that everything happens for a reason. People change so that you can learn to let go, things go wrong so that you appreciate them when they're right . . . and sometimes good things fall apart so better things can fall together.

The Buddhist view: Let go of control and our attachments to life.

Marilyn: Imperfection is beauty, madness is genius and it's better to be absolutely ridiculous than absolutely boring.

The Buddhist view: Be an individual; flow against the stream and social conventions.

Marilyn: I don't want to be wealthy; I just want to be wonderful.

The Buddhist view: Professional growth must be reinforced by personal growth.

Marilyn: We should all start to live before we get too old. Fear is stupid. So are regrets.

The Buddhist view: Don't worry about aging; focus on how you are living.

Marilyn: Give a girl the right shoes and she can conquer the world.

The Buddhist view: The eightfold path (right view; right intention; right speech; right action; right livelihood; right effort; right mindfulness; right concentration) is the Buddhists' "shoes," helping them stand firmly to deal with the world.

Marilyn: All little girls should be told they are pretty, even if they aren't.

The Buddhist view: See the best in everyone, helping them to recognize their Buddhist nature so they can evolve.

DAY **30**

USE YOUR DIPLOMA FOR GOOD

*Our ability to see is compromised when
ignorance puts a veil on our seeing power.*

~Pandit Rajmani Tigunait

There are far too many ignorant people in my town and probably
across the country and around the world. By "ignorant" I mean
they deprive themselves opportunities to be enlightened or, in
Christian language, to see the light. Let's think about what it is
that keeps a person continuously in an ignorant state. To help
with this concept, here are five characteristics of ignorance
according to Pandit Rajmani Tigunait, PhD, spiritual director of
the Himalayan Institute in Pennyslvania:

1. Ignorance, simply defined, is unwillingness to see or know
   anything other than what our habits have trained us to
   see and know.

2. Ignorance is an inner force driving us to see, find, know
   and experience what our ingrained habits demand that
   we see, find, know and experience.

3. Ignorance drives us to avoid the truth and reject any
   discovery of truth that conflicts with our habits and

conditioning. Ignorance is not passive; rather it is an active power pushing us to deny truth and continue to embrace our firmly and deeply conditioned habits and beliefs.

4. Ignorance swaps truth for falsehood, darkness for light, the unreal for the real.

5. Ignorance is so powerful that it gives us no alternatives but to align ourselves with our socially and culturally conditioned habits.

The way to remove ignorance is not complex. It merely involves permitting the light to enter. In fact, the word "enlightenment" contains within it the word "light."

Thus, defeating ignorance means acting upon the highest, most honorable and noble principles such as compassion, kindness, love, gentleness and other qualities similar to those. One recent powerful example of a person defeating ignorance and acting from the light comes via a man who, upon entering an oceanfront restaurant, noticed that the restaurant offered live lobsters. One lobster in the tank stood out because it was huge, weighing 17 pounds. The man immediately offered to purchase the lobster, asking that it be taken off the menu. Though it was a very expensive purchase, the man left the restaurant and released it into the ocean at a secret location. When asked about his action, the man explained that the lobster was approximately 80 years old and "deserved to live."

That's enlightenment! You, too, can break the power of ignorance and rise above it by paying attention to ingrained habits and beliefs and moving beyond them.

DAY **31**

HOW TO HANDLE CAMPUS FANATICS

The idea of propagating religion is outdated.
It no longer suits the times.

~Dalai Lama

Every college campus has a few enthusiastic Christians who seek converts. Perhaps you have been challenged or confronted by another student asking, "Are you saved?" or "Do you know the Lord?" Those questions are irritating because they are a predatory, intrusive action into your life. Consider the huge difference between predatory conversion and ethical conversion.

Predatory conversion:

- ❀ adherent driven by a sense that "others" are "lost" and doomed unless they are converted;

- ❀ is a tool of exclusive faith groups;

- ❀ there is a sense of victory and conquering over the "other";

- provision of humanitarian aid to vulnerable people (refugees, the sick, the poor) is not purely altruistic but a precondition to converting;

- comes from groups with a history of intolerance, supremacy, imperialism and violence;

- demands exclusive adherence.

Ethical conversion:

- seeker initiated;

- not rushed or forced but allows time for study, conversation and personal reflection before a decision is made;

- embraces freedom *of* religion, including the right to freedom *from* religious intrusion and exploitation;

- embraces religious pluralism and religious freedom of choice.

In societies with a higher consciousness, there has been significant progress in removing discriminations based on race, ethnicity, age, religion, gender, sexual orientation or physical disability. The logical next step is to curtail and eliminate predatory conversion. Freedom of religion includes freedom from religion.

DAY **32**

STOP COMPETING WITH CLASSMATES

People suffer because they are caught in their views. As soon as we release those views, we are free and we don't suffer anymore.

~Thich Nhat Hanh

The Buddha consistently taught that emotions such as anger, resentment and bitterness are poisons and obstacles to enlightenment. As soon as they arise, they must be dealt with in constructive and skillful ways. One such poison is lack of forgiveness. A pathway toward forgiving is offered by Clarissa Pinkola Estes in her book *Women Who Run With the Wolves*. She cites these four stages for arriving at complete forgiveness:

1. Forgo. Take a break from thinking about the person or event for a while.

2. Forebear. Abstain from punishing, neither thinking about it nor acting on (the offense) in small or large ways. Give a bit of grace to the situation.

3. Forget. To refuse to dwell, to let go, loosen one's hold, particularly on memory. To forget is an active—not passive—endeavor.

4. Forgive. A conscious decision to cease to harbor resentment, which includes forgiving a debt and giving up one's resolve to retaliate.

Today think about someone who has irritated or even injured you. Using the memory of the event, work your own way through these four stages.

DAY **33**

SHOW YOUR COLLEGE SPIRIT

The more we care for the happiness of others,
the greater is our own sense of well-being.

~Dalai Lama

A study done by researchers Ellen J. Langer and Judith Rodin demonstrated the truth of the Dalai Lama's teaching that showing love, kindness and compassion is self-beneficial. Furthermore, Langer and Rodin's study also revealed that those who do this live longer than those who do not!

Their study was done with elderly nursing home residents. There were two control groups, both of whom were given a box of small plants. The first group was told, "The plants are yours to have and keep in your room and take care of as you'd like." The second group was also all given a box of small plants and told, "The plants are yours to have and keep in your room. The staff will water and care for them for you."

Ellen Langer reported, "A year and a half later, we found that members of the first group were more cheerful, active, and alert, based on a variety of tests we had administered both before and after the experiment. Allowing for the fact that they were all elderly and quite frail at the start, we were pleased that they were also much healthier." In addition, Langer and Rodin were surprised to discover that there were twice as many deaths in the non-care group than the one which was responsible for looking after their plants. Langer also noted there was a clear connection between mind and body, that when "the mind is in a truly healthy place, the body would be as well."

GRADUATING—WITH HONORS

Cleverness is not wisdom.

~Euripides

The Oxford Dictionary of English defines wisdom as "the quality of having experience, knowledge, and good judgment." That's a fine definition. Comedian Jeff Foxworthy says something similar: "Wisdom equals knowledge plus scars."

So, how do you get wisdom?

Here are the seven ways:

1. Want it enough to seek it out and at any cost.

2. Read the writings of wise women and men.

3. Learn from mistakes, especially the bad, unpleasant, embarrassing ones.

4. Get up every time you fall down.

5. Learn from a teacher, mentor, guru, spiritual friend or anyone who is wise.

6. Wait for it, and be patient because wisdom comes cumulatively.

7. Be worthy of it!

DAY **35**

PULLING ALL-NIGHTERS

To shape your life begin by shaping your mind.

~Victor M. Parachin

The great *Dhammapada*, a highly regarded Buddhist scripture
that records the teachings of the Buddha, begins with this
wisdom:

> *We are what we think.*
> *All that we are arises with our thoughts.*
> *With our thoughts we make the world.*
> *Speak and act with an impure mind*
> *And trouble will follow you*
> *As the wheel follows the ox that draws the cart.*

> *We are what we think.*
> *All that we are arises with our thoughts.*
> *With our thoughts we make the world.*
> *Speak or act with a pure mind*
> *And happiness will follow you*
> *As your shadow, unshakable.*

In this teaching, the Buddha reminds us that our mind can be our greatest friend or our greatest foe. To shape your life, begin by shaping your mind.

DAY **36**

SLAY YOUR ORAL PRESENTATION

*My fear and doubts have vanished like mist into
the distance, never to disturb me again.*

~Milarepa

Many people hold themselves back and end up living a timid,
cautious, hesitant life because of fear. That may be why author
E. Stanley Jones said "fear is the sand in the machinery of life."
Today, overcome a fear. That's best done by taking action to
confront it as directly as possible. Remember than you can feel
the fear, *but take action anyway*. This lesson can be seen through
an experience from Maurice Chevalier, the French actor and
singer. At the height of his profession he suffered a near career-
ending moment. As he was stepping on stage to perform, he was
seized with nervousness so powerful he could not recall his lines.
Stammering and stumbling through, other actors had to cover for
him. This went on night after night.

Troubled and deeply concerned with his health, his
acting career and his future, he consulted with a doctor who
prescribed a rest period at a small town in southern France.

After a few weeks, the doctor visited Chevalier, suggesting he give a performance to the people of the village at the town hall. Chevalier protested, "I can't. I'm terrified. What if my mind goes blank again?" His physician responded, "There are no guarantees, but you must find a way to challenge the fear. Don't use it as an excuse not to act."

Chevalier performed publicly and perfectly. He would remember his doctor's words on many future occasions when he experienced doubts and moments of fear. Chevalier's action shows the wisdom of Ralph Waldo Emerson's insight: "Do the thing you fear and the death of fear is certain."

DAY **37**

WHEN YOUR PARENTS COME TO VISIT

With our thoughts we make the world.

~Buddha

Sometimes a parent will say to a child who is being disrespectful, "Watch your mouth." However, before any words come out of the mouth, they have first made their way into the mind as thoughts. That's why Buddhism summarizes character of development this way:

Thoughts become words;
Words become deeds;
Deeds develop habits;
Habits develop character.

This process begins in the mind with what we think. That's why it is vital for us to watch our mind, to be certain that what is in there is positive, kind, good, compassionate, honorable, noble, gentle and more. When that's not done, here's what can happen:

Angry thoughts become angry words;
Angry words become angry deeds;

Angry deeds develop angry habits;
Angry habits develop an angry character.

Each one of us can and should make a concerted, intentional effort to monitor the mind. When the negative enters, ask it to leave. It's just that simple.

DAY **38**

KEEP THE BACKPACK LIGHT

There will be calmness, tranquility, when
one is free from external objects.

~Bruce Lee

During the season of heavy rains, a village where the dwellers were known to be strong swimmers flooded as the river expanded. Six friends in the village decided to take a boat across the river to higher, dry ground.

Just as they reached the middle of the river, the boat stuck a floating tree and began to fall apart. Since all of them could swim well, they jumped out and began swimming to the bank. One friend, however, was struggling and swimming slowly, though he was known to be among the best swimmers in the village.

"Are you all right?" asked one of his friends. "You are swimming very slowly."

"Yes, I am all right, but I have a sack with a thousand coins tied around my waist, and they are weighing me down."

"Get rid of them," shouted the friend. "The river currents are swift and strong. Drop the sack."

gh the man was by now obviously exhausted, he shook
saying, "I've worked all my life for this money."

all of his friends reached the shore, they stood there
pleading with him: "Release the money belt. It's not worth it.
You're not going to make it!"

Their friend refused, was swept away with the current, and
his body never recovered.

This story is, on the one hand, very simplistic. Yet, if we
allow this story to be a metaphor for the way many people live,
it teaches this powerful lesson: We must never allow material
desires to weigh us down. Many people find themselves
"drowning" because they cling to expensive homes, luxury cars,
bulging closets, exotic vacations, etc.

Of course, it's important to have enough money to cover the
basic needs of life. However, it is worth reminding yourself that
needs can be met but desires are insatiable. To maintain inner
peace, balance and harmony in your life, you must have a right
relationship toward materialism. Happiness equals wealth is a
false equation. To be happy focus not on the accumulation of
wealth, but upon decreasing desire.

DAY **39**

COLLEGE ISN'T EASY: REWARD YOUR SUCCESSES

We should be happy to be born as human beings.

~K. Sri Dhammananda

The Christian doctrine of original sin is not directly found in the Bible. Rather it began as an invention of theologians beginning in the third century (CE) and culminating with Augustine in the fourth century. Simply stated, it says that every human being is born—through no fault of their own—a sinner and destined for eternal punishment (hell). The only antidote is a savior, someone else who has died and atoned for collective human guilt and sin.

This odd doctrine is absent in Judaism and Islam. And in Buddhist thought, it is rejected completely as "a theological fiction." Here's how Buddhist teacher K. Sri Dhammananda explains it:

> *The Buddha did not regard evil as something to be atoned for through a savior, but a defilement arising from ignorance which has to be outgrown through wisdom. He rejected as a theological fiction, the belief that man*

is cursed by a God born in sin, shaped in iniquity, and destined to a miserable eternity.

He goes on to note that "every person has the capacity for the pursuit of goodness, and even the most vicious person can by his or her own effort become a most virtuous being."

The Buddhist concept is that we all have the ability to live skillfully. The key is to access our innate inner wisdom, and the tool for doing that is the mind. Your thoughts and how you think can be constructive or destructive. One single thought can set you off into the direction of happiness or into the arms of difficulty, disappointment and despair. Thus, Buddhism stresses the vital importance of mind or mental training. This is done via meditation to develop thoughts of compassion and wisdom, for yourself, for other beings and for all of life. In this way you cultivate your highest virtues and your greatest humanity.

DAY **40**

WHEN YOUR ROOMMATES TALK BEHIND YOUR BACK

Do what you feel in your heart to be right,
for you'll be criticized anyway.

~Eleanor Roosevelt

A man and his son were taking a donkey to the market. As they were walking, some people saw them, saying, "Look at those fools walking when they could be riding the donkey." The father heard this and asked his son to ride the donkey while he walked alongside.

Before long, an older woman, seeing this, remarked, "What is the world coming to? Look at the young man riding comfortably while his elderly father is walking." Hearing that, the young man got down and the father rode the donkey.

As they went along, a young woman saw them and said, "You know, both of you should be riding the donkey." So the father joined his son on the donkey's back.

A little further down the road, a group of people saw them and said, "That poor animal is being forced to carry those two lazy men. Some people are so cruel."

Fed up with the criticism, the two dismounted and decided to carry the donkey instead, hoping this would silence all criticism. However, people simply stared and said, "Look at those two fools carrying the donkey."

The lesson in this story conveys these two basic truths: First, there is no escaping criticism. Second, it is impossible to please everyone. If you wither under criticism, you get lost in life. And if you try to please everyone, you end up pleasing no one.

GOLDIE HAWN AND THE BUDDHA

This world is swept away by aging, by illness, by death. No shelters exist...Make merit while alive.

~Buddha

The Buddha did not shy away from reminding people that as soon as we are born the aging process begins and does not reverse. Eventually, everyone will die.

On one occasion, the Buddha was engaged in a conversation with his closest companion, Ananada, who said, "It is amazing. It is astounding, how one's complexion is no longer so clear and bright; how limbs become flabby and wrinkled; how one's back, bent forward; there's a discernible change in one's faculties—the faculty of the eye, the faculty of the ear, the faculty of the nose, the faculty of the tongue, the faculty of the body."

"That's just the way it is, Ananada," said the Buddha. "When young, one is subject to aging; when healthy, subject to illness; when alive, subject to death. The complexion is no longer so clear and bright; the limbs are flabby and wrinkled; the back, bent forward; there is a discernible change in the faculties—the faculty of the eye, the faculty of the ear, the faculty of the nose, the faculty of the tongue, the faculty of the body. Those who live to a hundred are all headed to an end in death."

Of course, the Buddha was not being morbid nor pessimistic. He saw life as it really is and taught others to do the same. If we know that our time here is brief and limited, then there is chance that we will choose to make the most of our lives. Actress Goldie Hawn captures this Buddhist teaching in a simple, straightforward manner. She says, "Everybody ages. Everybody dies. There is no turning back the clock. So the question in life becomes: what are you going to do while you're here?"

DAY **42**

THE BUSY STUDENT'S 5-MINUTE BREATHING EXERCISE

The wise one who knows Breath thus…becomes immortal.

~Prashna Upanishad 3:11

One of Aesop's famous fables is this one about the tortoise and the hare. In that tale, the speedy hare constantly boasted how fast he could run. Tired of hearing him boast, the tortoise, named Slow and Steady, challenged him to a race. All the animals in the forest gathered to watch. As expected, the hare took off, leaving tortoise way behind. After a while, the hare became tired and decided to rest alongside the road, where he fell asleep, thinking, "There is plenty of time to relax." Slow and Steady walked and walked. He never, ever stopped until he came to the finish line. The animals who were watching cheered so loudly for Slow and Steady, they woke up Hare. Hare stretched and yawned and began to run again, but it was too late. The tortoise was over the line.

The traditional interpretation of this story is that the tortoise won simply because he was "slow and steady." Consider, however, a deeper meaning for this story, one about the breath. At the start, the hare rushed out, taking the lead. Though the normal breathing rate of a hare tends to be around 55 breaths per minute, it was certainly breathing more rapidly because of the effort expended. Both running and rapid breathing wear the body out quickly, so the hare was forced to rest and regain breath control. The erratic breathing pattern and the need for rest caused the hare to lose the race.

On the other hand, the tortoise, which takes one to three breaths per minute, started the race slowly, managing to maintain his steady pace throughout. Because he walked normally and maintained his normal breath pattern, he completed the course without exhaustion. Consider also this interesting statistic: A hare takes 55 breaths per minute and has an average lifespan of 10 years. A tortoise takes one to three breaths per minute and has an average lifespan of 190 years.

That observation led to the theory in India that one's lifespan can be measured not in years but in breaths. Deeper, longer inhalations and exhalations produce a healthy body and mind while poor respiratory habits lead to chronic, stress-related health issues. Here's a simple Buddhist breath exercise in three steps: First, inhale a complete breath through the nose. Second, hold that breath for a few seconds. Third, shape your lips as though you are going to whistle and then slowly exhale a complete breath through the mouth. Repeat this pattern for five minutes.

DAY **43**

LET GO OF BAD RELATIONSHIPS

Grasping at things can only yield one of two results:
Either the thing you are grasping at disappears, or you
yourself disappear. It is only a matter of which occurs first.

~S. N. Goenka

An environmental scientist working in Alaska witnessed a battle taking place on a river. As he walked along the short, he observed a magnificent, large salmon leaping in and out of the water. It was enjoying itself in the warm sun. What the superb creature did not notice was a bald eagle soaring high above. The majestic bird's sharp eyesight was also aware of the salmon. Totally oblivious of the dark shadow rapidly descending toward it, the eagle silently swooped in sinking its knife sharp talons into the salmon's back.

Then a furious battle erupted. The fish flapped and swam desperately attempting to dislodge the eagle. At the same time, the bird flapped its six-foot wings frantically trying to lift the fish out of the water. The eagle was able only to do so for a few seconds at a time before the fish was able to pull back into the river.

As the battle raged, it became obvious to the scientist that the eagle was growing tired but refused to unlock it talons. Finally, the salmon pulled the regal bird lower and lower into the water where its flapping wings were useless. Eventually, all the scientist could see was the white dome of the eagle's head slowly disappear into the river. Then the water's surface stilled.

Here's the sad part: to survive all the eagle had to do was *let go*.

That story is a metaphor about attachments. How often do we sink our "talons" into something or someone only to discover the attachment begins to sink us. We are far too easily attached to our expectations—expectations of ourselves and expectations of others. Buddhism teaches that attachment is dangerous because it constitutes an exaggerated sense of importance to something or someone. Non-attachment means loving but not grasping, enjoying but not possessing, appreciating but not gripping. Remember to release and relinquish.

DAY **44**

TAKE A DIFFERENT ROUTE TO CLASS

Sometimes full; sometimes half full.

~Zen Koan

Shunryu Suzuki, who was influential in establishing Zen Buddhism in America, tells of a lesson he learned while studying at a Zen temple in Japan. One of his tasks was to bring tea to his teacher. The first time he did this, he filled the small cup half full. This is the traditional way because Japanese teacups are handleless. When the cup is half full, it will not be too hot to hold.

However, his teacher reprimanded him, saying, "I don't care what the traditional way is, I want my teacup filled to the brim."

From then on, Suzuki poured tea that way.

One day a guest visited the temple and Suzuki served tea as he had been instructed—filled to the top. This time his teacher reprimanded him strongly, shouting, "A teacup should only be half full. Aren't you concerned that our guest will burn her fingers?" His teacher then instructed Suzuki to meditate on this koan (a koan is a riddle used to instruct): "Sometimes full; sometimes half full."

Though Zen masters have a justifiable reputation for being unpredictable and inconsistent, in this case he was trying to stress the importance of mindfulness. One definition of mindfulness can better help understand this incident: mindfulness is paying attention to the present moment with curiosity and kindness.

Suzuki was on automatic pilot. His Zen master correctly observed he simply did the same thing, the same way that he always did. However, Suzuki did not factor in that the guest, used to sipping tea the traditional way with the cup half full, could easily have burned her fingers at picking up the cup. Furthermore, with the cup full, she also may have spilled the hot liquid on herself.

Thinking about this Zen koan, "sometimes full; sometimes half full," examine your own personality and style. When do you operate on automatic pilot? When are the times you need to apply more flexibility or mindfulness, and see a person or situation with the concept of "sometimes full; sometimes half full"?

DAY **45**

DON'T BE A HATER

Every person who is born is born with an ax in his mouth.

~Sutta Nipata

The Buddha compares speech to an ax in this saying. In his day, an ax was not just a device for chopping wood, but a fine tool used to cut long planks of wood, shaving them smoothly for construction. Of course, an ax could also be used as a weapon for maiming or killing. With these words, the Buddha was reminding people to use their words to heal not hurt, to bring peace not pain. Harsh words are harmful, and all beings feel their effect, even animals.

One Buddhist teacher tells of a family dog, a large husky who was fascinated by animals on television. When they would appear, he would view them, sometimes barking at them and even biting at the television screen. One day when he saw animals on the television, he sat down directly in front of the screen, blocking the view of a family member who shouted at him to get out of the way. Because the tone was strong, loud and harsh, the husky reacted by going into the basement. For nearly a week, he remained there, coming up only to go outside to relieve himself. As soon as he entered the house, he retreated back into the basement. It was only when the family began to plead with him in gentle, soft, loving tones that he rejoined them upstairs.

Kind, compassionate, welcoming and warm language is something that is appreciated by all beings. That's why in the *Sutta Nipata* the Buddha added this additional wisdom about our words:

> *Speak kind words, words*
> *rejoiced at and welcomed,*
> *words that bear ill will to none;*
> *always speak kindly to others.*

LOVE YOUR HATERS

*True compassion does not come from wanting to
help out those less fortunate than ourselves but
from realizing our kinship with all beings.*

~Pema Chodron

We humans have the odd ability to separate ourselves from
others. We make judgments. We see, too easily, differences
and distinctions between ourselves and others. Every time this
happens, compassion is discounted and decreased.

However, when we learn to see commonality and unity of all
people, then our compassion is enlarged and expanded. Rather
than judging, try seeing others as just like you. Tell yourself we're
all the same and want the same basic things in life.

To deepen your compassion, banish artificial separation
between "us and them." Do this by repeating these affirmations:

Just like me, this person is seeking happiness.
Just like me, this person wants a meaningful life.
Just like me, this person seeks to avoid suffering.
Just like me, this person wants to be accepted and loved.
Just like me, this person is trying to learn and grow in life.

Just like me, this person experiences sadness, wounds and loneliness.

Intentionally direct them toward family, friends, acquaintances and strangers—especially those individuals you find annoying and irritating.

DAY **47**

HOW TO TACKLE THE FRESHMAN 15

With realization of one's own potential and self-confidence in one's ability, one can build a better world.

~Dalai Lama

Bettering yourself is very, very easy. Here are 10 simple ways:

- ❀ Ask better questions.
- ❀ Make better choices.
- ❀ Have better friends.
- ❀ Eat better food.
- ❀ Read better books.
- ❀ Set better goals.
- ❀ Practice better listening.
- ❀ Find better role models.
- ❀ Apply better judgment.
- ❀ Finally, just be a better person!

Here is some wisdom about self-improvement from across the ages:

Let us strive to improve ourselves, for we cannot remain stationary; one either progresses or retrogrades.
—Madame du Deffand

Employ your time in improving yourself by other men's writings so that you shall come easily by what others have labored hard for.
—Socrates

People seldom improve when they have no other model but themselves to copy.
—Oliver Goldsmith

The greatest of faults, I should say, is to be conscious of none.
—Thomas Carlyle

DAY **48**

LEARNING TO ACCEPT COLLEGE SETBACKS

*Learn to wish that everything should
come to pass exactly as it does.*

~Epictetus

Recently, I invited a weekly meditation group that I facilitate to meditate on this Persian proverb: It is easier to wear sandals than cover the earth with carpets. Specifically, I asked the group to offer an answer in one of three ways:

1. What does the proverb mean?

2. Why was it necessary for someone to create this saying?

3. What would be a modern example of someone trying to "carpet" the world rather than simply put on sandals?

With that proverb in mind and the instructions, we all meditated for 15 minutes. The discussion that followed briefly was most informing. One woman said that carpeting the world so that it would meet our needs is highly impractical and impossible, that a more skillful approach lies in adjusting ourselves to the way life is rather than trying to make it be the way we wish it should be.

Another person linked the Persian proverb to the popular and modern "Serenity Prayer:"

God, grant me the serenity to accept the things I cannot change,
Courage to change the things I can,
And wisdom to know the difference.

This Persian proverb also appears in Buddhist literature in the form of this simple story: A pampered princess was walking barefoot in her father's kingdom when she stepped on a thorn, which caused her great pain. She demanded of her father's advisors that the entire kingdom be carpeted. Gently and kindly, one advisor encouraged to simply have a pair of sandals made for her feet.

That story is one intended to teach the truth of the Buddha's observation that we will suffer and be unhappy as long as we cling to our ideas about the way life should treat us rather than adjust to the way it actually is. Both the Persian proverb and the Buddhist tale were created as reminders that we need to respond to life's pains and pleasures in the most skillful ways possible. It's all about learning to accept college life as it is rather than clinging to the way we want life to be.

DAY **49**

GIVE PROPS TO YOUR VEGETARIAN PEERS

I became a vegetarian after realizing that animals feel afraid, cold, hungry and unhappy like we do. I feel very deeply about vegetarianism and the animal kingdom.

~Cesar Chavez

Cesar Chavez is well known as a labor activist who led a historic movement for the rights of American farm workers. What's less well known is that Chavez was also a vegetarian who came to this position based on animal rights.

Though born into a Catholic family, Chavez sounds very much like a Buddhist when it comes to compassion and extending that to *all* sentient beings. In 1992 (one year before his death), he received a Lifetime Achievement Award from IDA (In Defense of Animals). There, he explained his position:

"We need, in a special way, to work twice as hard to make all people understand that animals are fellow creatures, that we must protect them and love them as we love ourselves. And that's the basis for peace. The basis for peace is respecting all creatures. We cannot hope to have peace until we respect everyone—respect ourselves and respect animals and all living things. We know we cannot defend and be kind to animals until we stop exploiting them—exploiting them in the name of science, exploiting animals in the name of sport, exploiting animals in the name of fashion, and yes, exploiting animals in the name of food."

If Chavez did not formally embrace Buddhism, he does reflect this Buddhist principle: That human beings are not privileged nor do they (we) have a special place above and beyond the rest of life. This world has not been created specifically for the benefit and pleasure of human beings. The planet is to be a place of safety and security for all life. In Buddhism a foundational principle is *ahimsa*, or nonviolence. This concept prohibits bringing harm or death to any living being. That's why vegetarianism is taught and promoted by Buddhism.

DAY **50**

SWEARING OFF SWEARING

Skillful speech requires that you abstain from...
malicious words, harsh language.

~Bhante H. Gunaratana

Sometime ago at a retreat, I took a series of yoga classes with an amazing instructor. Though stronger and far more flexible than most of us, she led through the yoga sessions with compassion and grace. I was so impressed with her that, when the retreat ended and I returned home, I looked up her yoga blog, where I was stunned to read the high level of vulgarities she used in her writing.

While I am hardly a prude—I coached hockey for a decade with young men who routinely excelled in the use of vulgarities—I was both shocked and disappointed. Here's why: vulgar, coarse language violates the Buddhist principle of right speech, which is number three on the Buddha's Noble Eightfold Path. Buddhism teaches that vulgar language leaves negative imprints on our mind and they linger there long after the words are uttered.

Generally speaking, yogis, Buddhists and all people of goodwill should abstain from vulgar language for these kinds of reasons:

It is done out of anger and even hatred.

It comes from a mind which is not at peace.

It's a sign of verbal and moral weakness.

It's not joyful.

It's negative and harsh.

It's often hard to be around someone using vulgarities.

It's a powerful tool for anger and hostility.

It intensifies angry, hostile feelings.

It's immature.

It reveals a flawed character.

It offends people—more than you think.

It sets a bad example.

It is a sign of ignorance not enlightenment.

It gives a poor impression.

It hurts your reputation.

It can trigger angry, hostile acts.

Spiritual evolution always involves purification of the mind. Any habitual use of vulgarities should be a signal for anyone on a spiritual path to begin reducing and rejecting such talk. And consider this additional thought: it is impossible to imagine a Buddha (or a Christ) habitually using vulgarities.

KEEP YOUR CAREER PATH OPEN

Don't allow yourself be trapped in someone else's story. Learn to let go and live the life you want.

~Victor M. Parachin

An old Zen story tells of a Buddhist monk in a tree. His hands are tied behind his back; his feet are also tightly bound. He cannot get a grip on a branch with his hands or use his feet to gain a foothold. The man is hanging from a branch with his teeth.

Complicating his dilemma is the presence of another person who has come along. Recognizing that the man in the tree is a Buddhist monk, the person asks him: "Would you please teach me the Buddhist way?" If the monk opens his mouth to answer, he will fall out of the tree. If he keeps his mouth closed, he misses out on the very opportunity which brings energy, passion and meaning to his life. Either way, his life is at a complete standstill. He is trapped.

That Zen story is told to remind us that many of us are like the man in the tree. We have managed to tie up our arms, bind our legs and then cling desperately to something or someone, refusing to let go even when a life-renewing opportunity comes our way.

One example could be that of a man whose dream has been to be a novelist. The significant people around him—his family and friends—have criticized and persuaded him that a safer and more financially secure path would be to enter law school. He does so, becoming a lawyer and gaining employment with a large, prestigious law firm. He receives a huge salary, one which is out of reach for most people. Yet, he is terribly unhappy. The dream of becoming a novelist that brought passion and meaning to his life earlier emerges periodically. But the man has, metaphorically speaking, tied his hands to a profession that required years of study. He has bound his feet to the large salary offered by his employer. So he continues to cling to a branch with his teeth, afraid to let go and live the life he wants.

DAY **52**

10 QUESTIONS TO REDIRECT COLLEGE ANGST

If you refuse to accept anything but the best out of life, you very often get it.

~W. Somerset Maugham

Right view is a critical component of the Buddha's Noble Eightfold Path and, appropriately, it is number one on the list. However, sometimes, to develop right view, you need to engage in right asking. If you want to bring more happiness and joy into your life, try asking (and responding) to these 10 questions:

1. Can I realize I'm having a wonderful life?

2. Can I inhibit my inhibition?

3. Can I listen and observe without coming to a conclusion or a judgment?

4. Can I look at someone or something as if I were seeing it for the first time?

5. Can I look at someone or something as if I were seeing it for the last time?

6. Can I understand that life is a game to be played with skill and enthusiasm?

7. Can I be free to enjoy my life as it is, not how I wish it to be?

8. Can I live without being greedy for results?

9. Can I be satisfied with the journey, not the destination?

10. Can I leave my boat behind once I have crossed to the other shore?

MEDITATE BETWEEN CLASSES

*Religion is an insult to human dignity. With or
without it, you'd have good people doing good
things and evil people doing bad things. But for
good people to do bad things, it takes religion.*

~Steven Weinberg

The Buddhist answer to the question "Is there a god?" is neither
yes nor no. It's non-theistic because there is no way to really
know if god exists or not. For example, when a Buddhist teacher
is asked the god question, the response generally follows this
way: "Maybe god exists or maybe god does not exist. Leave it.
Our task is to learn how to live peacefully and compassionately."

But there is more to all of this. Consider the fact that the
Buddha lived in a time when belief in God was the dominant
view. It was supported and reinforced by thousands of volumes
of scriptures. In spite of that, the Buddha observed that people
in his day were not at peace and, in fact, there was a great deal
of strife and tension between them. As he thought about this
matter, these things became clear to him:

Belief in god does not automatically make people good.

Lack of believe in god does not make people automatically bad.

Belief in god did not and does not lead people to an underlying unity. In fact, it is too often just the opposite. Human history is filled with persecution driven by religion, by the very people who believe in god. This was sadly noted by author Jonathan Swift: "We have just enough religion to make us hate, but not enough to make us love one another."

So, the Buddha concluded that the question of god is irrelevant. It needs to be left alone, not argued for or against. Mere belief does not prevent humans from acting in negative and destructive ways. The Buddha skillfully avoided the inconclusive debate about God's existence, favoring a focus on something more important and practical. He taught that the path toward positive and constructive living is via mediation. It is only when one sits quietly that he or she can have a direct experience of ultimate truth. Such awareness can only come by turning inward and cultivating a clear, calm, tranquil mind.

Thus, rather than focus on belief in god, the Buddhist approach is to "leave that alone" and focus on meditation. It is through the methodical practice of meditation that people are universally empowered to develop a compassionate heart, a benevolent spirit and a peaceful mind.

DAY **54**

RESPONDING MODERATELY TO CAMPUS BULLIES

When angry, practice restraint; when greatly angry, practice greater restraint.

~Victor M. Parachin

When Buddhist meditation teacher B. H. Gunaratana was a little boy, he learned a lifelong lesson Gunaratana tells of a day growing up in Sri Lanka when he and some friends harassed his uncle's big, beautiful elephant by tossing small pebbles at her. They did this until she became frustrated and angry with them. The magnificent creature could easily have crushed the small boys if she so desired.

However, what she did was both remarkable and inspiring. After the boys had thrown pebbles at her, the elephant used her powerful trunk to pick up a branch about the thickness of a pencil. She used the branch to "spank" the boys by gently tapping them around the shoulders and back. The creature displayed amazing restraint, doing only what was necessary to get the boys attention about their unpleasant behavior.

For days after that incident, the elephant remained distant and unfriendly toward Gunaratana. It was obvious to him that her feelings were hurt and he, himself, was ashamed of his behavior. Wanting to make it up to the elephant, Gunaratana admitted to his uncle what he had done, and his uncle made a suggestion. He advised the boy to take the elephant to a nearby large creek and there, to gently scrub her skin with coconut shells while she relaxed and enjoyed the cool bath. After that, the elephant befriended Gunaratana.

Today, he tells his audiences to remember his uncle's elephant whenever they feel justified in reacting with violent anger and to respond with the same moderation as did the elephant.

DAY **55**

APPLY THE FOUR DEBTS OF GRATITUDE TO COLLEGE LIFE

Do not go about complaining how hard it is to live in this world. Such behavior is entirely unworthy of a real man.

~Nichiren Daishonin

On January 16, 1262, Japanese Buddhist monk Nichiren Daishonin, wrote a letter to a spiritual seeker in which he outlines what have come to be known as The Four Debts of Gratitude in Buddhism.

1. Debt of gratitude to all living beings.
2. Debt of gratitude to parents.
3. Debt of gratitude to government for peace.
4. Debt of gratitude to the Buddha.

Those Four Debts of Gratitude are universal and still applicable today for all people. Consider them in this light:

1. Debt of gratitude to all living beings. These include friends, family members and classmates who have helped us; animals that have brought us comfort and pleasure; all life forms—insects, birds, fishes—which maintain ecological balance making the planet habitable for all of us.

2. Debt of gratitude to parents. Regardless of whether parents were good or not, they did keep us alive as infants and care for us when we could not care for ourselves.

3. Debt of gratitude to government for peace. Think of places around the world where governments cannot keep the peace and there is civil war, hunger, suffering—where there are long lines of refugees and refugee camps.

4. Debt of gratitude to the Buddha. This includes all other spiritual teachers who shed light on our path, showing us how to live better lives and how to be better human beings.

Today, incorporate the Four Debts of Gratitude into your life as a college student.

DAY **56**
FITNESS MOTIVATION

*While it is usually easy to detect the symptoms of a
physical disease, we often remain ignorant of psychological
diseases. They follow us like a shadow. When we do
not examine the constructs of our mind with wisdom
and awareness, then poor psychological health follows.*

~Hsing Yun

A friend of mine who is a specialist on health and nutrition
recently raised this question: What is good health? Answering
her own question, she said that health is not merely being free
of a disease or an illness. To illustrate her point, she asks these
provocative questions:

- Are you healthy just because you are not in the hospital?

- Are you healthy just because you are not under the care
  of doctor?

- Are you healthy if you have too much stress in your life?

- Are you healthy if you are mentally or emotionally
  ungrounded?

- Are you healthy if you lack meaningful relationships and connection with other people, friends and family?

- Are you healthy if you have a sedentary lifestyle and lack a physical outlet to move your body?

- Are you healthy if you don't enjoy your work, where you spend a large part of your day and time?

Good health, she says, is dependent upon maintaining proper balance of body, mind and spirit, as well as social and work life.

Buddhism has a similar medical theory, namely, that body and mind are interdependent. A healthy mind leads to a healthy body. A healthy body influences the health of the mind. A healthy body becomes our tool for cultivating clarity of mind and compassion of heart. With a clear mind, the result of meditative practices, we are able to become profoundly self-aware, analyze ourselves, see clearly the issues and work skillfully to resolve them.

It is always periodically worth asking yourself, "Am I healthy?" If the answer is yes, then express gratitude. If the answer is no, then take the necessary steps toward health.

BUDDHA U

DAY **57**

LISTEN TO YOUR ROOMMATE'S PROBLEMS

*Teach this triple truth to all: A generous heart,
kind speech, and a life of service and compassion
are the things which renew humanity.*

~Buddha

The Buddha taught there are three ways to make the planet a better place: having a generous heart, engaging in kind speech, and living a life of service and compassion. He called this teaching "a triple truth." It is not an accident that the "triple truth" begins with generosity. It is a generous heart out of which come kind speech and a life of service and compassion. The spiritual practice of *dana*, the Pali word for generosity, is based on this triple truth.

Consider these questions to help you deepen your own practice of dana. Take your time going over these because your answers will be instructive, suggesting what you might want to change and what you might like to keep about how you give and, equally importantly, how you receive. Once you've gone over them, return to them in six months and see what has shifted for you.

- ❀ In what ways have you given recently and to whom?

- ❀ What do you find easiest and most enjoyable to give?

- ❀ What is most difficult for you to give?

- ❀ To whom is it easiest and most enjoyable to give?

- ❀ From whom is it easiest for you to receive?

- ❀ From whom is it hardest for you to receive?

- ❀ To whom are you able to give without expecting thanks or return?

- ❀ From whom are you able to receive without expectation of thanks or return?

- ❀ Do you feel indebtedness to people who give to you? Which ones? Why?

- ❀ Do you feel resentment at being asked to give? Why?

- ❀ Do you have past experiences which affect how you give and receive?

- ❀ Have there been times when you could give but held back? Why?

- ❀ Have you felt there were times when you gave too much or too little?

ONLY GET A PET YOU CAN TAKE CARE OF

Life is as dear to a mute creature as it is to man. Just as one wants happiness and fears pain, just as one wants to live and not die, so do other creatures.

~Dalai Lama

While all the world's religions stress the importance of compassion to other people, Buddhism is unique in that it teaches compassion for *all* beings: humans, animals, insects, worms, birds, etc. Even grasses and trees should be treated with respect and compassion.

Some of this Buddhist teaching has filtered into other religious traditions that have not been as quick to recognize the validity of compassion for animals. One example comes via a friend of mine who is a Christian minister. For several years now, he has offered an annual Bless the Pets service at his church. When he's questioned about this practice—and he is—he explains that human relationships are not the only ones that count in our world. He also notes that humans have erroneously considered themselves to be the only objects of God's love. This belief has been held at the expense of concern for the rest of nature and its inhabitants. The Bless the Pets event is a small reminder that other creatures are important, also. It is a tiny moment of rebellion against the misguided belief that humans are the only ones for whom God cares. It is a statement that God loves cats, dogs, birds, lizards and all the other animals that share the earth with us. And because God loves them, we should love them as well.

My pastor friend, sounding very Buddhist, goes on to enumerate these other reasons why all creatures are worthy of compassion:

- ❀ Pets in our lives rely upon us for nurturing and care, thus keeping us from focusing only on ourselves.

- ❀ Pets force us to understand that we live for others as well as ourselves.

- ❀ Pets remind us that we all interdependent, part of a vast web of relationships that form the fabric of our world.

- ❀ Pets also help us to see that life always involves both giving and receiving.

- ❀ Pets open our eyes to the fact that life is a process of caring and sharing.

Here is an ancient Christian prayer attributed to St. Basil the Great, which also teaches that animals are most worthy of our respect and compassion:

O God, enlarge within us the sense of fellowship with all living things,
our brothers the animals to whom you gave the earth as their home in common with us.

We remember with shame that in the past we have
   exercised the high dominion of man with ruthless
   cruelty so that the voice of the earth,
which should have gone up to Thee in song has been a
   groan of travail.
May we realize that they live not for us alone, but
   for themselves and for you and that they love the
   sweetness of life even as we, and serve
you better in their place than we in ours.

STUDY, STUDY, STUDY

*Patience is a sign of wisdom just as the ability to wait
for a desired result is an indicator of maturity.*

~Victor M. Parachin

Even though most of us wish to be further along and more
advanced in our life journey, this type of growth cannot be rushed
and when it is, the result is failure. Two parables indicate this
deep truth.

The first one is an ancient story which tells of a spiritual
master who knew a sacred mantra that could raise the dead.
Several of his senior students pleaded with him to share this
mantra. Though he refused for weeks, they continued to beg
him, saying that knowing this mantra would raise their level of
enlightenment. Finally, after badgering him for many months, the
master relented and shared with them the secret mantra. He
instructed them to be very careful in using it.

They were, of course, delighted. As they made their way
toward a nearby village, they saw a set of bleached animal bones
lying in the sun. Wanting to test the secret mantra, they stood
around the bones and recited it in unison. Suddenly the bones

took on flesh and a ferocious, angry tiger emerged, killing all of them.

The lesson in this ancient parable is that the senior students did not yet have the maturity, wisdom and skill to possess such knowledge. Those are qualities which cannot be rushed.

A second and more recent parable is told of a naturalist who observed a butterfly struggling to break out of its cocoon. It was an intense battle and the creature did not seem to be making progress. In order to assist, the naturalist used a pair of tiny scissors to gently cut the cocoon. The butterfly was then able to emerge, but it wings lacked color and were withered. The butterfly died a few hours later.

The lesson in this second story is the same as that of the ancient parable: Growth cannot be rushed. It can only be aborted.

So, be patient with yourself if you "haven't yet arrived." Give it time, do your practices, continue to learn and apply. When the time is right, you will arrive.

DAY **60**

WHEN YOU'RE BARELY PASSING HISTORY

*Remember that sometimes not getting what
you want is a wonderful stroke of luck.*

~Dalai Lama

Life is made up of frustrations. Whether they are large or small, they nevertheless test our patience and maturity. One skillful way to manage the feelings that emerge from a frustrating incident is to remind yourself that "sometimes not getting what you want is a wonderful stroke of luck."

An example of this is offered by Indra Devi, the woman who was instrumental in bringing yoga to the West and expanding its popularity. While living in India in the 1940s, she was writing her first book using a manual typewriter. A friend invited her to stay at his family estate near the Himalayas so that she would have more uninterrupted time to complete the manuscript. As was her daily custom, she rose just before sunrise for meditation outdoors. Going to her usual spot, she found it impossible to begin her pranayama (breath) exercises because heavy smoke was coming from the nearby kitchen where the staff was preparing breakfast.

After trying three different spots unsuccessfully, she finally retreated to a small garden, which was perfect except for a peacock living on the grounds. The bird was upset by her presence, making threatening sounds and gestures toward her. Thoroughly irritated by the frustrations of doing her morning meditation, she gave up and began walking back to her room. Suddenly she noticed sheets of white paper scattered on the hillside. When she picked them up, she let out an audible gasp because the papers were pages from her one and only manuscript. Evidently, the morning winds picked them up from her room, carrying them out of the open windows.

As she gathered them up, Devi "blessed the kitchen smoke, the unsuccessful meditation, and, of course, the peacock." Had she not given up on meditation because of the frustrating circumstances which came, the gardeners would have collected the papers and burned them that morning. "I could never have been able to reconstruct the manuscript. Thus there would have been no book," she says.

Based on that experience and many others, Devi often reminded people it is important to "learn not to let things upset us unduly. Everything that happens occurs for a reason."

DAY **61**

BE KIND TO THOSE BEYOND YOUR FRIEND CIRCLE

Just as a mother protects with her life her child, her only child, so with a boundless heart should one cherish all living beings radiating kindness over the entire world.

~Buddha

Consider this scene. You are walking through a forest with your teacher, your best friend, a colleague and your worst enemy. Suddenly, a heavily armed bandit emerges and threatens to kill all of you unless you choose one from the group to be sacrificed. Only then would the others be released to proceed.

Now, consider how you might respond.

You might say, "I choose myself. If I made any other choice I simply couldn't live with myself. Also, such a self-sacrificial act may have a positive impact upon the bandit."

You might say, "I choose my enemy. This isn't ideal but is the obvious choice for me."

You might say, "I choose my teacher. She is mature and highly evolved and most prepared for death."

You might say, "I choose my colleague. As I have neither ill will nor good will toward him, this will result in less karmic consequence to me."

You might say, "I cannot choose!" but the bandit demands you make a choice or all will perish.

When this riddle is presented to groups, very seldom is a best friend offered as a sacrifice. This indicates that most of the time, most of us naturally feel a deeper concern for someone we know and love than toward someone we feel more neutral about.

Yet, a core teaching of the Buddha is that we are to cultivate a "boundless heart, cherishing all living beings." The warmth and love we naturally feel for our family and friends is to be expanded. It's a noble goal. Perhaps this reminder from W. H. Auden can offer additional insight: "Love your crooked neighbor with all your crooked heart."

DAY **62**

THE ADVERSITY ADVANTAGE

Suffering also has its value.

~Shantideva

During the early months of World War II, Nazi submarines operating in wolf packs successfully sank an alarming number of British military and merchant ships. Hitler and the German high command were confident this tactic could blockade England, starving the British into submission and surrender.

In 1940 alone, the submarines sank 300 British ships, a number so high that Winston Churchill ordered the statistics to be withheld, fearing his nation's morale would sink. Because there were an appalling number of casualties, Churchill instructed the Royal Navy to determine what could be done to save more lives at sea.

While interviewing survivors, Navy officials made this fascinating discovery: older sailors had a much higher survival rate than did younger, newer recruits. This surprised Navy officials as they assumed that younger, more physically fit sailors would be more likely to survive an attack.

Probing further, they came to the conclusion that the older sailors had overcome more adversity in their lives than did the younger ones. Those experiences made them more resilient and gave them more confidence they could survive and that they would be rescued.

Thus, Shantideva, the eighth century Indian Buddhist scholar, rightly observed that adversity brings its own unique values and advantages. When you face unwelcome changes and challenges, don't become discouraged. Rather, greet them as teachers who can help you develop greater personal powers.

DAY **63**

KEEP YOUR DORM ROOM/ APARTMENT CLEAN

Accelerate the beautiful; abandon the unbeautiful.

~Victor M. Parachin

An interesting experiment was conducted in a poor section of a major city in Great Britain. Two streets, parallel to each other but one mile apart, were carefully selected by researchers. Both streets ran through a neighborhood with similar rates of unemployment, poverty and crime. Unbeknownst to the residents, one of the streets was secretly selected to be cleaned daily for a year and trash collected on a weekly basis. Gang graffiti was removed, and curbside areas were treated to flowering plants and bushes, which were watered regularly. In addition, repairs were made and maintained to street signs and lights. There was no public acknowledgment concerning the project of beautification.

One year later, the communities along the two streets were compared. Statistics clearly demonstrated that there was a 50 percent reduction in crime on the cleaned and adorned street.

Furthermore, residents living on that street exhibited more pride in their neighborhood.

Those two streets can serve as a metaphor for our lives. Within each one of us are two blocks: one which is beautiful and compelling; another which is impoverished and barren. It is up to us to accentuate the beautiful and abandon the unbeautiful. It is up to us whether we will focus on good conversation or unkind gossip; whether we will be optimistic and hopeful or negative and despairing; whether we will have spiritual friends who lift us up or people who lead us in circles or even astray. There are two streets running through your life. Choose which one to live on.

DAY **64**

TAP INTO COMPASSION—
ON YOUR BIRTHDAYS

A man is truly noble only when he has
compassion toward all living creatures.

~Buddha

A birthday is an auspicious occasion which we celebrate with gifts and a special meal. Interestingly, however, Buddhism offers an alternative view on birthdays. I first came across this in *Orthodox Chinese Buddhism* by Sheng Yen. He notes that according to worldly customs, people generally celebrate birthdays with parties, gifts, banquets, etc., but that this reveals an incorrect way of thinking.

In the Buddhist view, a birthday is a time to remember the birthday person's mother and her suffering in giving birth. "On this date, one should raise his feelings of appreciation for his mother to a higher level." This is done by thinking of all the kindness and effort it took on her part to give one birth and then carefully nurture an infant. "One should not remember one's day of birth with a hedonistic celebration," he states rather emphatically. The most appropriate way to "celebrate" is to perform acts of charity, such as releasing captive animals into nature and making financial donations to worthy organizations or needy individuals.

So, what should we do living here, in the West, where there are high expectations concerning birthdays? Perhaps find a middle way where the focus includes the birthday person as well as:

* helping another person who is in difficult circumstances (acts of kindness)

* purchasing a live fish or lobster from a food store/ aquarium and releasing

* giving a check to a charity or anonymously giving money to a poor individual, perhaps a community college student struggling financially

You can, of course, come up with your own creative ways of tapping into this compassionate way to celebrate your birthday.

DAY **65**

TUTOR A STRUGGLING PEER

If you cannot help others, at least do not harm them.

~Dalai Lama

One weekend fierce winds knocked over a beautiful, large tree in my yard. So, I called a man who is a certified arborist and tree remover. I've had him do work in the past because a) he loves trees; b) he is does good work at a fair price; and c) he is very wise, a Zen master in disguise, I believe.

Yet one more reason I like this man is because he employs people others will not. He told me his simple philosophy is this: When you see a man down, help him, *but then let go*!

He models that principle nicely as he hires those with criminal records, those with addiction issues, those who are deemed unemployable to others. This man gives them a chance and then lets go. It is up to them what they do with an opportunity to strengthen and stabilize their lives.

It's a good way for us to approach the delicate task of helping others, being sure that we empower people to break free of limitations. The simple principle of helping someone up and then letting go is a sound one.

WALKING AWAY FROM TOXIC "FRIENDS"

*When the student is ready the teacher appears but when
the student isn't ready the teacher must disappear.*

~Victor M. Parachin

Upon meeting a renowned horse trainer, the Buddha asked
him how he trained his horses. The trainer explained that some
horses respond to gentle training, others respond to harsh
training, and others require a combination of both harsh and
gentle training. At times a horse does not respond to either type
of training. In that case, the trainer said he would simply kill the
horse.

Then the trainer asked the Buddha how he trained his
students. The Buddha replied, "In the same way." Some students
respond to gentle criticism, others respond to harsh criticism,
and others to a mixture of the two. However, if a student didn't
respond to either type of criticism, he'd kill the student. This,
of course, shocked the horse trainer. (Perhaps the Buddha,
opposed to killing anything, wanted to shock him.) If the trainer
could kill a horse, why couldn't a teacher kill an unteachable

student? Perhaps the Buddha hoped the man would realize that life is precious to all beings. Nevertheless, the Buddha explained what he meant by using the word "killing." "If a student does not respond to gentle criticism or harsh criticism or a combination of the two, then I would no longer train the student, which essentially killed the student's opportunity to grow in practice."

The Buddha, like many of us, wanted to please people and worked hard at maintaining relationships. Some, however, cannot and should not be sustained. In essence, this exchange between the Buddha and a horse trainer is a healthy reminder that severing some relationships is okay. A common Eastern proverb notes: when the student is ready the teacher appears. The other side of that proverb is equally wise and true: when the student is not ready, then the teacher must disappear. Some people are simply not ready for your insight, your help, your wisdom or your friendship.

DAY **67**

10 WAYS TO ALLEVIATE ACADEMIC ANXIETY

*If we wish our nature to be free and joyous, we
should bring our activities into the same order.*

~Vinoba Bhave

1. Meditation

   *Meditation brings wisdom; lack of meditation leaves
   ignorance.*
   —Buddha

2. Yoga

   *Yoga is the only thing that has helped me realize the
   source of my self-destructive behavioral patterns and the
   need to take control and responsibility for the state of my
   mind and my actions.*
   —DW, Inmate, Mississippi Correctional Facility

3. Kindness

   *This is my simple religion. There is no need for temples;
   no need for complicated philosophy. Our own brain, our
   own heart is our temple; the philosophy is kindness.*
   —Dalai Lama

4. Tolerance

   Tolerance is giving to every other human being every right that you claim for yourself.
   —Robert Green Ingersoll

5. Mind management

   The power of the mind is in itself neither positive nor negative—it just is! It can work both ways, depending on where it is directed.
   —Indra Devi

6. Wisdom

   Know well what leads you forward and what holds you back. Choose the path that leads to wisdom.
   —Buddha

7. Self-improvement

   You are perfect as you are and you can use a little improvement.
   —Shunryu Suzuki

8. Nature

   Climb up on some hill at sunrise. Everybody needs perspective once in a while, and you'll find it there.
   —Robb Sagendorf

9. Patience

   Can you remain unmoving until the right action arises by itself?
   —The Tao

10. Spiritual friends

   We are like chameleons, we take our hue and the color of our moral character from those who are around us.
   —John Locke

DAY **68**

EXERCISING YOUR POWER OF CHOICE

To different minds, the same world is a hell, and a heaven.

~Ralph Waldo Emerson

At ten thirty in the evening, a woman was working alone at a gas and convenience store. Though normally quiet at that time, the store had a line of people waiting to pay for purchases. In the line was a man, obviously becoming impatient. As she rang up his purchases, he began to berate her for "being so slow" and for the store not having more people at the registers. The woman, upset at his tone and demeanor, made an error ringing up his purchase. She had to do it a second time, which only further agitated the customer, who said, "Can't you do your job properly? Hurry up so I can get home!" The woman concluded the sale and gave the man his change. As he left, he looked back at her, shouting, "You're a useless employee. In the morning I'm going to call the manager and get you fired."

A few moments later, another customer came. He had been sitting in the car of the man who was angry and saw what transpired. That man made a small purchase and, at the register, said to the distraught woman, "I am really sorry about him and can make no excuse for his behavior. I'm making this small purchase so he doesn't know what I'm doing, but here is a tip for your service this evening." He gave the astonished woman a fifty-dollar bill and left quietly.

That story is worth analyzing. Why is the first man so clearly calloused and cruel while the second man is clearly compassionate and kind? What is it about people which takes them over to the dark side or strengthens their resolve to remain firmly centered as benevolent and charitable individuals?

Clearly, it comes down to making a choice. Moment by moment and day by day, compassion is an intentional choice originating in the mind. Depending on where you direct the mind, you can choose to be calloused and cruel or compassionate and kind. It's just that simple.

DAY **69**

REMOVE THAT INNER NEGATIVITY

We are already pure and good inside—
that is our basic nature.

~Tara Springett

Unfortunately, too many people spend too much time listening to inner negativity. Here's a partial list of negative inner chatter. See how many of these have entered your mind just over the last day or two:

- I'm not smart enough.

- I'm not good enough.

- I'm not talented enough.

- I'm not thin enough.

- I'm not rich enough.

- I'm not secure enough.

- I'm not worthy enough.

- I'm not fast enough.

❀ I'm not committed enough.

❀ I'm not attractive enough.

❀ I'm not driven enough.

❀ I'm not successful enough.

❀ I'm not educated enough.

❀ I'm not confident enough.

❀ I'm not brave enough.

❀ I'm not happy enough.

This list is quite incomplete as human beings have an amazing ability for negative inner thought and chatter. Part of this is due to the scarcity culture in which we live, which is constantly reminding us that we are inadequate. This aspect of our culture successfully fuels the creation of our deepest fears.

Put an end to this inner negativity by shifting your focus to this Buddhist psychology which teaches that our inner nature is pure inner goodness and inner wisdom. It is not accessed because it is covered up and buried under our negative thinking. Just as those who seek better physical health give up junk food, we need to establish better mental and emotional health by giving up "junk thoughts." So, today, stop thinking and saying such terrible things about yourself. Be mindful of the Buddha's own teaching: "You, yourself, as much as anybody in the entire universe, deserve your love and affection."

FIND LIKE-MINDED FRIENDS

*Buddhism is inherently practical. It is a way of
knowledge that is gained by firsthand experience.*

~Roger Housden

More and more, Buddhism is establishing itself as a powerful,
permanent presence in the West. Among its many appealing
qualities is the fact that it is more a psychology than it is a
religion. Unlike the religions people in the West are familiar with,
Buddhism is based on logic and reason, not faith and blind belief.

The Buddha himself stressed the practical and the logical
when he said, "Do not be satisfied with hearsay or with tradition.
When you know in yourselves these ideas are unprofitable, then
you should abandon them. When you know in yourselves these
things are profitable, then you should practice and abide by
them."

Buddhism is a simple and practical psychology that works
ideally in daily life. In his very first teaching offered at Deer Park
in Isipatana, India, the Buddha expressed these basic Four Noble
Truths:

1. Everyone suffers.

2. All suffering has a cause.

3. That cause can be terminated.

4. The tool for termination is following the Noble Eightfold Path.

And the eightfold path is a simple system of "rights": right understanding, right intention, right speech, right action, right work, right effort, right thinking, right meditation.

Committing to and joining with others traveling along the Noble Eightfold Path deepens and enriches one's life. Those who have turned to the teachings of the Buddha say they are drawn to Buddhism because of its teachings on mindfulness, non-harming, mind management, compassion toward all sentient beings, and the fact that it is a logical and reasonable way to live.

DAY **71**

LEARNING FROM THE MAN WHO GRABBED HIS TESTICLES

You shouldn't be attached to thoughts or run
after illusions, but rather let them go.

~Taisen Deshimaru

Zen masters tell this unusual story about a man who is dreaming that he is walking down the street. It is a winter evening. Suddenly he sees a pouch full of coins on the ground. He tries to take hold of it, but it is frozen in the ice.

In order to free the pouch, he urinates all around it to melt the ice. Once again he grabs the pouch with both hands. He feels pain intense enough to wake him up. When his eyes open, he sees the ceiling of his bedroom, not the starry skies of winter. His testicles are firmly clutched in his hand and aching painfully. Furthermore, his mattress is soaked!

This odd story (Zen masters love to use weird stories to make a point) offers two important lessons. First, when we don't see the difference between an illusion in our life and the reality of our life, we can end up in pain and deeply embarrassed.

Second, we need to be careful about our desires and dreams. Of course, we all have dreams or goals we think we *must* attain—career success, wealth, marriage, family, etc. However, as we focus on those dreams and desires, there is a tendency to blow them completely out of proportion to reality. For example, for years a friend of mine dreamed of owning a luxury German vehicle. One day he found just the right one at just the right price. He bought it immediately. Within weeks he discovered that it was a major gas guzzler and was extremely expensive to maintain. Even a simple oil change cost nearly four times more than one for his previous vehicle. While it was pleasant to drive, it cost him a great deal more to operate. In the end, he got what he wanted, but it was a painful ownership. His overriding desire for the automobile blinded him to the reality of owning one.

Uncontrolled desire combined with the inability to distinguish illusion from reality can only bring you pain, embarrassment and disappointment.

KEEP THINGS SIMPLE

Preserve the natural state.

~Buddhist Proverb

Three monks were walking along a dusty path. They saw a man standing on the top of a hill ahead.

The first monk said, "He must be standing on top of the hill looking for his straying cattle."

The second monk said, "No, I think he's standing on top of the hill because he was separated from his traveling companion and is looking for him."

The third monk said, "Most likely he's standing on top of the hill to enjoy the pleasant breeze and the magnificent view."

Arguing a bit and unable to agree, the three monks climbed the hill and asked the man, "Are you standing on top of this hill to look for your cattle or to find your companion or to simply enjoy the breeze and view?"

To their question, the man replied, "No. I'm just standing on top of this hill!"

Too often we add complexity to the simplicity of life. That's why Buddhism stresses the importance of preserving the natural state. Don't complicate your life. Keep it simple!

DAY **73**

ENLIGHTENED ENOUGH!

To achieve wisdom is to be enlightened.

~Sheng-yen

After the attack on Pearl Harbor on December 7, 1941, the American government forced 120,000 Japanese Americans on the West Coast out of their homes and businesses into internment camps for the duration of the war. One of those individuals was Al Tsukamoto, whose parents arrived in the United States in 1904.

Tsukamoto owned and operated a fruit farm in California. Rather than simply abandon the family farm and see the business destroyed, Tsukamoto looked for a compassionate American who would help him. This was not easy to do as Pearl Harbor had just been bombed by the Japanese, placing anger toward those of Japanese ancestry at an all-time high. Tsukamoto remembered on American who had always been friendly, respectful and courteous. He was a young man in his early thirties named Bob Fletcher, a farm inspector for the State of California. Tsukamoto approached Fletcher with a business proposal: If he were willing to operate the family farm, pay the taxes and pay the mortgage while the Tsukamoto family were confined, in return, he could keep all the profits.

Fletcher agreed, quit his job and for the next three years worked 18-hour days operating a fruit farm. Faithfully, he paid the taxes and kept up with the mortgage payments. Fletcher kept only half the profits as his salary. Though Tsukamoto told him to live in his family house, Fletcher stayed in the bunkhouse Tsukamoto had built for migrant workers. Each week, he cleaned and maintained the Tsukamoto residence while waiting for their return.

Whereas most Japanese American families lost their property and businesses while they were in camps, Tsukamoto came back in 1945 to discover he had money in a bank because Fletcher deposited half the profits into the account. Fletcher's willingness to help the Tsukamoto family brought him both ridicule and scorn from other Americans in the area. He remained indifferent to criticism, saying he felt Japanese Americans were being mistreated.

Fletcher's attitude and actions are indicative of a person who is enlightened enough. "To achieve wisdom is to be enlightened," says Zen master Sheng-yen. When we think of enlightenment, too often we think of famous spiritual leaders such as the Buddha or the Dalai Lama. That line of thinking simply places enlightenment out of reach. Sheng-yen's description of enlightenment as wisdom is an accurate one and within our grasp. Just like Bob Fletcher, you have the capacity to think, feel, speak and act out of wisdom. That's enlightened enough!

DAY **74**

STUDYING IN DESIGNER CLOTHES

*As an arrow maker whittles and creates straight
arrows, so a master directs his straying thoughts.*

~Buddha

One of the many remarkable Tibetan refugees is Gelek
Rimpoche. He was born in 1939 and recognized as an incarnate
lama at the age of four. After receiving a rigorous Buddhist
education comparable to a Western PhD in philosophy, he began
to teach. When the Chinese invaded Tibet, Gelek Rimpoche was
one of the last to flee Tibet in 1959. Though he was a high-
ranking Buddhist teacher, he had to leave everything behind—his
status, his family, his aides, his books, his clothing, even his
horse. Upon arrival in India, he was granted refugee status.
Unemployed for some time, he finally found employment for All
India Radio in Delhi as well as the India National Archives as a
curator of Tibetan titles. Because of his training and skill, he was
asked to establish Buddhist teaching centers in the West, first in
Netherlands and, more recently, in Ann Arbor, Michigan.

Today, he teaches around the world. Following a lecture in Hong Kong in which he talked about being on a spiritual path, he was approached by a man who said he liked the talk and wanted to be on a spiritual path. "But does that mean I will have to give up my Rolls Royce?" the man asked. Rimpoche answered wisely, "As long as you drive the Rolls Royce, you are okay. But when the Rolls Royce starts driving you, you're in trouble."

The truth is that you can enjoy material prosperity as long as you drive your desires rather than have them drive you. The same is true of the mind. It is a very good thing to have a strong, active mind and imagination. However, you must manage the mind and imagination rather than have them manage you.

DAY **75**

EVERY DAY IS A GOOD DAY!

*Sunshine is delicious, rain is refreshing, wind braces us
up, snow is exhilarating; there is really no such thing
as bad weather, only different kinds of good weather.*

~John Ruskin

One day Banzan (1619–1691) was walking through a busy
market when he happened to overhear a conversation between a
butcher and his customer.

"Give me the best piece of meat you have," said the
customer.

"Everything in my shop is the best," replied the butcher. "You
cannot find any piece of meat here that is not the best."

Upon hearing those words, Banzan became enlightened.

Now consider what exactly Banzan experienced when he
heard the butcher's answer to the customer? There are a couple
of ways to interpret this story. One is to see that every moment
is the best moment because it is the only moment we have.
Understanding that is enlightenment. Another way of connecting
to this story is via the observation of John Ruskin:

"There is really no such thing as bad weather, only different kinds of good weather."

In other words, view every day that you have as a very good day, the very best.

DAY 76

VOLUNTEER AT A LOCAL SOUP KITCHEN

We never give up on anyone.

~Chogyam Trungpa

Before Pervez Musharraf became president of Pakistan, he was an officer in the army. One of his assignments was to lead a Pakistani battalion as part of a UN peacekeeping force in Bosnia. As a commanding officer, he was given housing inside the compound of a grand palace. The first evening there, Musharraf was walking the grounds when he heard the distinct sound of voices pleading outside the walls.

Asking what the sounds were, he was told it was a nightly event. Then he was taken to the main entrance gate to the grounds, where he saw some two dozen children crying and begging for food. His eyes filled with tears at the sight, and he felt helpless.

Though he could not solve the problem of hunger in Bosnia, Musharraf did give the children all the money he had on him. And when his group of three battalions arrived in Bosnia, he explained this situation. Upon learning of the children's cries for food, the men in all battalions agreed to fast one day every week, distributing the food they had saved among the needy of Bosnia.

Their noble gesture is a reminder to all of us that whenever we see suffering of any kind, we should do what we can to alleviate some of it. Never give in to despair. Never give up on anyone.

DAY **77**

SURVIVING YOUR FIRST COLLEGE BREAK-UP

You are today where your thoughts have brought you;
you will be tomorrow where your thoughts take you.

~James Allen

One of England's most prominent physicians was Dr. Bruce Bruce-Porter, who practiced in London. One of his patients was a young girl who had a life-threatening illness. That young woman was mesmerized by a serialized fiction story carried in the newspaper, in which the heroine had the same condition. She so identified with the girl in the story that she would become like her after reading an installment. If the heroine was happy, Dr. Bruce-Porter's patient was happy. If the heroine was sad, Dr. Bruce-Porter's patient was equally sad. As the story's plot progressed, the heroine's condition worsened day by day. So did the patient's. That change was noticed by Dr. Bruce-Porter, who became alarmed at the possibility that if the heroine in the story died, so would his young patient.

The physician tracked down the author, who told him that he had killed the heroine off in the final installment, which was not yet published. Dr. Bruce-Porter explained, saying, "I am sure when my patient reads the final installment, she too will die. Would you change it and give her a chance at recovery?" The author readily agreed. The young girl, encouraged by the bounce-back of the heroine, developed hope and recovered from her illness.

Across the ages, sages and saints have reminded us about the power of our mind. The Buddha taught "the mind is everything. What we think we become." Poet John Milton accurately described the power of our thoughts saying, "The mind…can make a heaven out of hell, a hell out of heaven."

What's on your mind?

Is your mind filled fear, fright, hesitation and doubt, or are you using your mind to maintain thoughts of confidence, optimism, hope and trust?

How you think is up you. You have the power. Use it.

DAY **78**

WORK WITH YOUR PEERS TOWARD COMMON GOALS

*Compassion is not having any hesitation
to reflect your light on things.*

~Chogyam Trungpa

Perhaps your personality isn't the kind to become a true social radical, but could you consider working with others who want to create social transformation on the planet? To do this is a form of compassion.

For motivation, consider these elements of the life of the Buddha:

* Born to wealth, he abandoned family and luxury to pursue a spiritual path.

* After experiencing enlightenment, he crisscrossed (by foot) Northern India and parts of Southeast Asia, teaching.

* His orange robe was made from discarded cloth often found in garbage dumps. Usable bits of material were

selected, washed and dyed orange partially because that was the color of clothing worn by convicts in his day.

❀ He established communities that were clear alternatives to the rigid caste system of his day (and one which by birth he was destined to rule).

❀ Becoming a monk or nun meant taking vows promising never to refer to your previous caste.

❀ Monastics shaved their heads and wore simple robes, making it hard to distinguish gender, wealth or caste.

❀ They begged for food from all castes. This irritated the top Brahman class because their food was mixed with food from "untouchables."

❀ As they walked all over Asia, the Buddha and his companions wore distinctive robes, thereby becoming a walking advertisement for this new path offered freely to all.

As you evolve, grow and mature, consider adding into the mix of your life ways you can help create a gentle, kinder, more compassionate environment.

DAY **79**

AVOID LABELING

*Nothing in your experience—your thoughts, feelings or
sensations—is fixed and unchangeable as it appears.*

~Yongey Mingyur Rinpoche

A simple experiment involving the letter "T" was conducted
with subjects. The letter was carefully drawn so that both the
horizontal and the vertical lines were exactly equal in length.
When the subjects were asked whether one of the two lines
was longer than the other or of equal length, three different
responses were offered. And the responses given were based on
the subject's geographical background.

Those who lived mainly in flat plains, such as Nebraska,
tended to see the horizontal line as longer. This was due to the
fact that their eyes were accustomed to seeing wide expanses
of flatland. By contrast, those living mainly in mountainous areas,
such as Colorado, were overwhelmingly convinced that the
vertical line was longer. This was due to the fact that their eyes
were accustomed to seeing terrain in terms of up and down. Only
a small group of the subjects recognized the two lines as being
equal.

This experiment shows that perception may not be reality. Furthermore, it reveals that perception is filtered and altered by our experiences. That is actually good news for this reason: if you feel trapped by perceptions about the way your life is and has to be, those perceptions can be changed and adjusted to reality.

Here are some examples:

- ✹ If you perceive yourself as hesitant and timid, change that perception and see yourself as courageous and bold.

- ✹ If you perceive yourself as incapable of sustaining a marriage or other significant relationship, change that perception and see yourself as fully competent to commit and sustain a relationship.

- ✹ If you perceive yourself as unable to succeed in some aspect of life, change that perception and see yourself as having the ability and drive to achieve success.

- ✹ If you are filled with self-loathing, change that perception and see yourself as being able to practice self-love.

KEEPING THE EGO IN CHECK

Happy are those who have overcome their egos.

~Buddha

Patrul Rinpoche (1808–1887) was a highly regarded Tibetan lama. He had an impressive education combined with personal charisma and the ability to teach complex matters in a simple, straightforward way. Something of a wandering ascetic, whenever he settled for a few weeks, students and local villagers gathered around him for instruction. Patrul Rinpoche did not like the attention and adulation that was offered to him, so he would often leave an area.

After leaving yet another town because of this, he entered a village where he asked a family for a place to stay. The mother agreed to let him stay, but only if he worked as the family servant. Rinpoche readily agreed. His tasks included sweeping the floor, emptying the nightly urine pots and other chores. A few days later, a group of Buddhist monks arrived there, inquiring of the mother whether a prominent lama was in the area. She asked for a description of the lama and upon discovering he was her servant, the woman was greatly embarrassed.

That story is very popular among Buddhist monks because of the great humility which this deeply learned and talented monk exhibited. Patrul Rinpoche provides a powerful example for today because humility is an increasingly rare virtue on the planet. Egos are overinflated and out of control. This can be seen by the rudeness that is often exhibited by customers toward workers in service fields such as retail and restaurants.

Each one of us should intentionally cultivate humility by respecting all others and treating them as we would want to be treated.

FUNNY BUDDHIST LESSONS

*Find common ground between the teachings of Islam
and of Buddhism. On the basis of this common ground,
followers of each tradition may come to appreciate
the spiritual truths their different paths entail.*

~Dalai Lama

Mullah Nasruddin was a thirteenth century Sufi (Islamic) visionary and mystic joker. He was able to convey deep truth via humor. He was acquainted with Buddhist teachings as some of his stories are adapted from Buddhist tales. Here are a few sample stories, along with Buddhist interpretation, from this remarkable and unusual mystic:

> *Nasruddin was chatting with a neighbor when
> Nasruddin's son came up the road holding a chicken.
> "Where did you get that chicken?" Nasruddin asked. "I
> stole it!" said his son. Turning to his neighbor, Nasruddin
> proudly said, "That's my boy. He may steal, but he won't
> lie."*

Buddhist perspective: Virtues must be consistent.

*One day Nasruddin went into his favorite coffee shop
(not a Starbucks!) and said, "The moon is more useful
than the sun." The owner of the shop asked, "Why?"
Nasruddin replied, "We need the light more during the
night than during the day."*

Buddhist perspective: We must practice and learn when
life is easy so that the lessons can be applied when life is hard.

*A friend asked Nasruddin, "How old are you?"
"Fifty," he replied.
"But you said the same thing two years ago!" his friend
responded.
"Yes," replied Nasruddin. "I always stand by what I've
said."*

Buddhist perspective: Right speech.

*Bragging to a friend, Nasruddin said, "When I was in the
desert, I caused an entire tribe of warriors to run."
"How in the world did you do that?" asked his friend.
"Easy," said Nasruddin, "I just ran and they ran after me."*

Buddhist perspective: Life is interpreted and understood
according to our perspective.

DAY **82**

BECOME MORE COMPASSIONATE: SIX STEPS FOR THE COLLEGE STUDENT

Selfless compassion is like rain. It falls on everything and does not discriminate.

~Sheng-yen

Compassion is powerfully absent on our planet. Correct this. Intentionally begin developing and accentuating compassion within yourself. Here are six steps:

1. Know yourself. Be honest about your strengths and weaknesses—about what evokes negative emotions and what evokes positive emotions in you.

2. Maximize the positive aspects of your personality. Minimize the negative ones.

3. View every person you meet with kindness and sympathy.

4. Forgive people for their mistakes and foolishness.

5. Be concerned about others' pains and hurts.

6. Respond to them in appropriate ways through your words and deeds.

Becoming compassionate is easy! The trick is simply to do it.

DAY **83**

GO AHEAD AND DOUBT

*Doubt is good. But doubt with an open mind that
is willing to learn, grow, evolve and expand.*

~Victor M. Parachin

In one of the Buddhist sutras (scriptures), a group of people visited the Buddha with this concern: "Many teachers come through our village. Each teacher has his own doctrine. Each teacher claims his particular philosophy and practice is the truth. However, some of these teachings contradict each other. This is all very confusing for us. What should we do?"

The Buddha responded with understanding: "It is indeed confusing and it is understandable why you are troubled." Then, he offered this advice: "Do not take anything on trust merely because it has passed down through tradition, or because your teachers say it, or because your elders have taught you, or because it's written in some famous scripture. When you have seen it and experienced it for yourself to be right and true, then you can accept it."

That is remarkable advice from a religious leader. Essentially, the Buddha is minimizing trust and maximizing doubt. In fact, he applied this same principle to his own teachings when he famously said, "Believe nothing, no matter where you read it, or who said it, no matter if I have said it, unless it agrees with your own reason and your own common sense." The Buddha is stressing the importance of doubt over blind faith. However, doubt should also be infused with an open mind.

An example of this approach is offered by Buddhist nun Jetsunma Tenzin Palmo, who says of herself: "Even now, after all these years, I still find certain things in the Tibetan dharma that I'm not sure about at all." She brought this issue to her teacher, who offered this wisdom: "That's fine. Obviously, you don't really have a connection with that particular doctrine. It doesn't matter. Just put it aside. Don't say, 'No, it's not true.' Just say, 'At this point, my mind does not embrace this.' Maybe later you'll appreciate it, or maybe you won't. It's not important."

Doubt is good but do your doubting with an open mind that is willing to learn, grow, evolve and expand.

DAY **84**

STOP JUDGING

*As compassion grows stronger, so does the willingness
to commit yourself to the welfare of all beings.*

~Dalai Lama

In his book *How to Expand Love*, the Dalai Lama offers a
personal example of how compassion can be done in an
unbalanced way:

> *From childhood I have had a tendency toward love and
> compassion, but it was biased. When two dogs were
> fighting, I would have strong feelings for the one who
> lost. Even when two bugs fought, I had strong concern
> for the smaller one, but would be angry at the winner.
> That shows that my love and compassion were biased.*

Of course the Dalai Lama is not alone in the way he feels
compassion. All of us naturally feel the greatest compassion
for those closest to us, for those we love and, like the Dalai
Lama, tend to feel compassion for the poor over the wealthy, for
children over adults, for the weak over the strong.

That's why Buddhism offers this five-step exercise to cultivate a balanced compassion, especially for people we don't know well or may not even like. Here are the five steps:

- 🏵 Step 1: This person is a fellow human being, just like me.

- 🏵 Step 2: This person has feelings, thoughts, emotions, just like me.

- 🏵 Step 3: This person has experienced joy and sadness, just like me.

- 🏵 Step 4: This person has had physical and emotional hurts, just like me.

- 🏵 Step 5: This person wishes to free of pain and suffering and desires to be happy, healthy and loved, just like me.

DAY **85**

CONTROLLING FEAR

Real control lies in the mind.

~Franz Metcalf

Ajahn Brahm, the abbot of a Buddhist Center near Perth, Australia, tells about a monastery member who has very bad teeth. Many of them needed to be extracted, but the monk didn't like the effects of a local anesthetic so, after considerable research, found a dentist who was willing to do a tooth extraction without an anesthetic. Understandably, this very thought can bring fear and pain to the mind.

One day, however, the monk was seen outside the monastery workshop. He was holding a freshly pulled tooth in the claws of an ordinary pair of pliers. Quite shocked by this, he was asked how he managed to pull his own tooth. His answer amplifies the quote from Franz Metcalf, "Real control lies in the mind."

The monk explained that going to the dentist involved a huge amount of effort and time. He needed to find a ride to the dentist's office in Perth. The return trip itself took nearly two hours along with the hour or so in the dentist's office. An entire afternoon or morning was used up just to have one's tooth extracted without a local anesthetic. It was all very inconvenient.

So on this occasion the monk decided to save himself time by doing it himself: "When I decided to pull out my own tooth, that didn't hurt. When I walked to the workshop, that didn't hurt. When I picked up the pair of pliers that didn't hurt. When I held the tooth in the grip of pliers, that didn't hurt either. When I wiggled the pliers and pulled it, it did hurt then, but only for a couple of seconds. Once the tooth was out, it didn't hurt much at all. There was only five seconds of pain, that's all."

The lesson to reflect on from this monk's experience is this: *Fear heightens pain*. While some fears are healthy and necessary for survival, many fears are unhealthy. Then the result is that they control and consume us. The antidote to fear is the mind. Use it to control the fear.

YOU ARE GOOD ENOUGH

*Buddhism is not properly a religion because
it de-emphasizes faith in the unknown and
unknowable and it rejects dogmatism.*

~Robert F. Spencer

Jesus taught: "Do to others what you would have them do to you" (Matthew 7:12). In this verse, there is no mention of God because there is no need of a God to live this noble way.

Furthermore, the Buddha showed that a person can indeed be good without God. The Buddha taught that:

- People can live confidently and be moral without a belief in immortality.
- People can live a righteous life without any help from a divine authority and law-giver.
- People can live an honorable way of life without rites and rituals.
- People can lead a noble life without depending on a divinity to give them salvation.

❀ People can find liberation or enlightenment without religion.

❀ People can follow high ideals without being made to feel guilt or fear.

❀ People can introduce others to this gentle, compassionate way of life without forcing or threatening them.

❀ People can teach others to lead a compassionate life without superstitious beliefs, irrational dogmas and emotional manipulation.

❀ People can have a belief system based on reason, not blind faith.

Yes, the Buddha (and Jesus) teach that one can be good without God, and that's good enough.

DAY **87**

IT'S ALL GOOD

Heat and cold, the wind and rain, sickness,
prison, beatings—I will not fret about such things
for doing so will aggravate my trouble.

~Shantideva

When Akbar the Great (1542–1605) became Ruler of India, he inherited his father's trusted advisor Birbal. However, he was uncertain of Birbal's loyalty and irritated by Birbal's unending optimism. Birbal constantly stressed that everything happens for a reason and for a good purpose. "It's all good!" he would say.

While sharpening his sword, Akbar accidentally cut off half of one finger. Seeing that, Birbal again reminded the ruler not to be upset because all things work out for the best. "It's all good!" he told Akbar.

Upon hearing that, Akbar became angry and misused his power by ordering Birbal to be arrested and jailed. Because of the pain in his hand, Akbar decided to distract himself by going into the forest to hunt. There, he became separated from his guards and was captured by a primitive forest tribe. They took him to their priest, suggesting he be offered as a human sacrifice to please the gods. When the temple priest examined Akbar, he told the tribe this captive could not be used for sacrifice because their rituals called for a perfect specimen. This captive had half a finger missing. So, he was released.

Akbar returned to his palace, where he immediately prayed, thanking God for letting him cut off half a finger and thus sparing his very life. Furthermore, he went to the prison, where he apologized to Birbal and asked, "Now I do understand how my injury was for the best, but please explain to me, why did God allow me to imprison you? How is it for the best that you are here due only to my anger? How could it be said of your situation, 'It's all good?'"

"This is easy to answer," said Birbal. "Had you not jailed me, I would most likely have been with you on the hunt. We would both have been captured and when the forest people rejected you as their sacrifice, they would certainly have found me to be a perfectly acceptable sacrifice."

That legend simply suggests that everything which comes our way is an important part of our evolution, expansion and growth. Everything—the good, the bad, the ugly—comes with that potential. It's all good!

DAY **88**

PRACTICE RANDOM ACTS OF KINDNESS

The guru—dispeller of darkness.

~Georg Feuerstein

The word "guru" comes from two Sanskrit words: *guha*, which means cave, and *ru*, which means light. Combined, guru simply means someone who brings light to the cave. This is, in fact, one standard definition of a guru as "transmitter of light."

Here's a meditation to do on the word guru. First, sit quietly and identify those who have brought light to your cave. Pause and silently express gratitude to those individuals living or deceased. Second, continue to sit quietly and identify people you know whose cave needs light. Offer this Buddhist loving kindness meditation:

May (name) be happy.

May (name) be healthy.

May (name) be safe.

May (name) be free of suffering.

End your meditation by considering how you could be the person who can bring light to their cave. What form would that light take, a text or email of encouragement? An invitation to join you for tea, coffee and conversation? An opportunity to walk and talk together? A kind expression of your ongoing love and support?

Consider this true encounter related by a woman in a letter to an advice columnist. She wrote to share how a simple act of kindness impacted her life. The woman signed her letter only as "Slimming Fast in Florida" and explained she is one of those "oversized" people who more than fills an airline seat. While on an airplane, which was filled nearly to capacity, a "good-looking gentleman" sat down in the seat directly beside her. He greeted her with a friendly "good morning" and flashed a warm smile. As he buckled his seat belt, he said to the woman, "I always feel cramped in these seats. Would you mind if I raised the armrest between us?" Slimming Fast in Florida knew he didn't feel cramped. "He obviously wanted to make sure I was more comfortable." As they chatted briefly, the man complimented the woman on her hairstyle and the "lovely dress" she was wearing. "His remarks had a lasting effect on me," the woman said, adding that since that flight, she has lost twenty-three pounds "thanks to a gentleman who didn't scowl at an overweight woman," but instead extended her his kindness. His courtesies and acts of kindness clearly brought light to her cave!

DAY **89**

HOW TO HANDLE FAILURE

Do what you can, the best way you can, and then move on.

~Victor M. Parachin

Among the many titles given to the Buddha is this unusual one: *The teacher of those who can be taught.*

It points to the reality that even the Buddha faced limits when dealing with people. History clearly demonstrates that the Buddha was a highly effective teacher, *but not all the time*. At one Buddhist monastery, there was great discord combined with a complete lack of harmony. There, the monks bickered and fought with each other constantly. One group, for example, accused the others of not following the rules. The accused denied it, counter-accusing the others of violating monastic rules by making false accusations.

When the Buddha learned about the discord, he personally visited. After listening carefully to both sides, he offered these recommendations:

🏵 that all the monks apologize to each other for
   misunderstandings;

* that they refrain from complaining, criticizing and condemning;

* that they seek to work diligently, maintaining harmony and good will.

Though his suggestions are most reasonable, they elicited yet more arguments and disagreements among the monks. It soon became clear to the Buddha that this group of people were not honestly open to resolving differences. So, he thanked them for their hospitality and left content that he had tried his best, but that it was to no avail.

This is a useful story for several reasons. First, it shows that, in this case, not even the Buddha could bring people together and develop harmony. Second, it shows us how to respond when we are dealing with difficult people. Like the Buddha you are to do our best to develop goodwill and concord. However, when people are resistant and refuse to participate that way, then, like the Buddha, you should move on with no regrets, no anxiety, no dis-ease.

DAY **90**

KNOWING WHEN TO
HOLD YOUR TONGUE

The only real valuable thing is intuition.

~Albert Einstein

koan—a paradox to be meditated upon
that is used to train Zen Buddhist monks to abandon
ultimate dependence on reason and to force them
into gaining sudden intuitive enlightenment

I lead a meditation group every Wednesday evening for an hour.
Midway through, we hear a koan, meditate on it and then discuss
it. Here is one koan that was used:

When you meet a master swordsman,
show him your sword.
When you meet a man who is not a poet,
do not show him your poem.

Here were some of the responses to the koan:

❋ As the sword is a weapon, it would make sense to reveal
   to another person with a sword that you, too, are armed
   and able to prevent them from taking the advantage.

❀ A woman who is a published poet herself explained that showing your poem to a person who is not a poet puts that person on the spot. That person can be embarrassed, intimidated, or feel awkward reading and commenting on a poem when they don't know much about poetry. So, don't put a non-poet into an uncomfortable situation by "showing off" your poem to them.

❀ Showing a sword to a swordsman and not showing a poem to a non-poet can be taken to mean: do and say the right thing, in the right way, at the right time, to the right person. It's about being totally in the present moment.

Perhaps you have a different interpretation of this koan. That's because there is no single "right" answer to a koan. Their purpose is to break us from the bad habit of relying completely on reason and move toward an intuitive understanding. Reason provides information; intuition provides insight. In the Zen tradition, intuition is regarded as the most valid source of insight and wisdom.

DAY **91**

DON'T BE AFRAID TO LEAD

May I be a lamp in the darkness.

~Shantideva

Bodhi means enlightenment and *sattva* refers to someone who has the courage and confidence to attain enlightenment, using it to benefit all other beings.

One way the word *bodhisattva* can be translated into English is by the word "hero." Thus, a bodhisattva is a spiritual hero, someone who is a fighter. Such an individual fights with him or herself, overcoming negative, hostile, unskillful thoughts and emotions.

That individual then helps others overcome lack of compassion, intolerance, stupidity and other mean-spirited aspects of society and culture. A bodhisattva is an individual who has a tenacious grip on the desire to reach out and help other people. It is the expression of the ninth century Indian Buddhist teacher Shantideva who said, "May I be a lamp in the darkness." It is the reminder of Jesus who told his followers, "You are the light of the world."

Some well-known contemporary bodhisattvas are Thich Nhat Hanh, Albert Schweitzer, Mother Teresa and the Dalai Lama. There are many whose lives are invisible to the larger public.

You may know one of them.

You may be one of them.

Why not?

THE JOYS OF GENEROSITY

*If you knew, as I do, the power of giving, you would
not let a single meal pass without sharing some of it.*

~Buddha

A dictionary definition of generosity reads this way: the quality
of being kind, understanding, and not selfish; the quality of
being generous; especially, willingness to give money and other
valuable things to others.

Buddhist tradition notes that the Buddha himself taught
there are three fundamental types of generosity.

First there is material generosity, which involves sharing
money and other material things with others.

Second, there is emotional generosity, which the Buddha
described as "making others feel unafraid." We do this when we
spend time with a person who has just experienced a traumatic
event such as the diagnosis of a life-threatening illness, loss of a
loved one or loss of a job.

Third, there is the generosity of sharing wisdom with others,
such as leading a meditation group, offering a spiritual workshop,
or making a presentation about higher values and ethics.

The Buddha often taught about the importance of generosity because it is not only helpful to the recipient of our generosity but we, ourselves, are greatly helped when we act generously. Generosity is a powerful virtue because it helps us counteract four Buddhist poisons: clinging, guarding, clasping and attaching. When we are generous, we free ourselves from that grasping and let go. Gandhi wisely said, "The fragrance remains in the hand that gives the rose."

Bottom line: via generosity you free others from suffering and you free yourself from suffering.

DAY **93**

WORK HARD, PLAY HARD

Cultivate the fine art of balance; balancing mind
with heart and the spiritual with the practical.

~Victor M. Parachin

An American writer tells of visiting the Dalai Lama in Dharamsala, India. While there, he was invited to meditate with the monks. Rising at three thirty in the morning for the first meditation round, the man meditated and was doing well until, an hour later, hunger pangs emerged. Dedicated to the meditation practice, he worked to ignore them, assuming that this material concern had no place in the midst of a spiritual practice.

His assumption was quite incorrect, and he realized that when less than few minutes later, a basket of freshly baked bread made its way down the silent line of meditators. That was followed by a jar of peanut butter with a single knife. All the meditators ate a breakfast of bread and peanut butter in communal silence. Then, they promptly resumed formal meditation practice.

The writer learned that the pragmatic approach to monastic life came directly from the Dalai Lama. His philosophy is that the journey toward higher consciousness can be combined with practicality. That approach reflects a proper balance between mind and heart, between the material and the spiritual. It is a balance which is often absent in the lives of many. Cultivate this balance to live with daily happiness and joy.

DAY **94**

HOW TO USE MALA BEADS TO STOP WORRYING

*As rain does not break into a well-thatched house, so
craving does not break into a well-trained mind.*

~The Dhammapada

Buddhist monks do not have many possessions but one item
they all have and carry is mala beads. These are similar to
Catholic prayer beads and are used by Buddhists as a way of
focusing the mind for mediation. The Dalai Lama is seldom seen
without his beads. Here's how Buddhist monks came to use mala
beads.

According an ancient legend, King Vaidunya consulted
with the Buddha about his life's worries and stresses. "Over
the last few years disease and famine have swept my country.
The people are struggling, distressed. It is something I worry
about day and night without any relief. My people and I are in a
desperate situation. Buddhist doctrine is far too profound and
extensive for us to study and practice given our circumstances.
Please teach me the essence of your teaching so that I may
practice it and teach it to my people."

The Buddha responded: "King Vaidunya, if you want to eliminate worry and anxiety, make a circular string of 108 bodhi seeds, carrying them always. Use them to recite—*I take refuge in the Buddha; I take refuge in the dharma; I take refuge in the Sangha.* Count one bead with each recitation of these three." This is the earliest story concerning Buddhist mala practice. (This has come to be known as taking refuge in the three jewels: the Buddha, the dharma, the sangha.)

Though it is universally practiced by Buddhist monks, it is clear from this story that the Buddha's lesson about mala beads was first directed to lay people to deal with the daily pressures and stresses of life.

Consider this practice for yourself when anxious and worried: Here is an updated way of using Mala beads. As you touch one, say to yourself:

The Buddha is my example (This human being found release from suffering)

The Buddhas teachings will guide me.

The spiritual community will inspire me.

Count one bead with each recitation of those three phrases. Do it 108 times. Observe the effect upon yourself when you are through.

DAY **95**

COMPASSION IS THE BEST REVENGE

Great compassion penetrates into the marrow
of the bone. It supports all living beings.

~Nagarjuna

When Zen master Bankei (1622–1693) held a weeks-long
meditation retreat, pupils from many parts of Japan attended. At
that retreat, one of the students was caught stealing. The issue
was brought before Bankei with the request that the culprit be
expelled.

Bankei ignored the request and continued the retreat.

A few days later, the pupil was caught stealing a second
time and the matter was brought to Bankei, once again with the
insistence the pupil be dismissed. Again, Bankei disregarded
the matter. That angered the students who circulated a petition
demanding the thief be expelled, stating that otherwise, they
would all abandon the retreat.

After reading their petition, Bankei called for a group
meeting. "You exhibit great wisdom," he told them. "You know
right from wrong." Then he said, "You may go somewhere else to

study if you wish, but this poor brother does not even know right from wrong. Who will teach him if I do not? I am going to allow him to stay here even if all the rest of you leave."

Two things happened. First, the man who had stolen began to weep and all desire to steal vanished. Second, and to their credit, the other pupils understood the importance of compassion over justice. They remained in the retreat with Bankei.

While not every wrong can be overlooked, ignored or dismissed, some can be treated with compassion rather than the harsh hand of legalism. Consider a strikingly similar story to that of Bankei, except from recent times.

A security camera in a Nervous Dog Coffee shop in Ohio recorded a customer stealing the contents of the employee tip jar. Store employees could have called the police. They could have filed charges. They could have made sure the thief was prosecuted. They could have ensured that he would have a criminal record history, making it difficult to pass a background check for future employment.

To their credit, the store employees did something completely unexpected and totally compassionate. Meeting together amongst themselves and the store managers, the group, knowing that many people in their state were struggling because of the weak economy, held a food drive for the thief.

While no one can predict whether or not the man would ever steal again in the future, it is certain that their act of kindness would be permanently etched in his mind.

DAY **96**

RETHINK YOUR FEAR
OF SPIDERS

*Generally, everyone feels compassion, but the compassion
is flawed. In what way? We measure it out. For
instance, some feel compassion for human beings but
not for animals and other types of sentient beings.*

~Khenchen Thrangu Rinpoche

A woman tells of a private meeting with a high-ranking Tibetan
Buddhist monk. The Rinpoche—that is an honorary title of
respect given to one who is recognized as a reincarnated or
accomplished teacher of Buddhism—poured her a cup of tea.

As they talked and sipped tea together, a fly inadvertently
landed in her tea. Because the woman had lived in India for some
time, she was accustomed and unaffected by insects. Though
the fly in her tea was a minor occurrence, her face did register
that something was amiss. When the Rinpoche asked what was
wrong, she replied, "Nothing really. Just a fly in my tea."

Quite concerned, the Rinpoche rose from his chair, glanced
at her cup of tea and, with deep concern, placed his finger into
the tea. With great care he gently lifted out the offending fly and

carried him out of the room. Upon returning, the Rinpoche was beaming proudly, saying, "The fly will be all right." He explained that he had placed the fly on a leaf of a branch by a plant near the door, where he could dry off his wings. The Rinpoche was delighted to see that the fly was alive and quickly began fanning his wings, drying them so that he could take flight.

The woman says she remembers little of the conversation that day but remembers a great deal about the Rinpoche's breadth of compassion for all beings, including a tiny fly.

His actions are a welcome minority opinion to the actions exhibited too often in our own culture, which thinks nothing about destroying insect lives with chemical sprays or fly swatters, or simply crushing them on sight.

The powerful lesson she will always remember is that all living beings—just like human beings—want to be happy and free of suffering.

DAY **97**

BUILDING COMMUNITY

*Strive at first to meditate upon the
sameness of yourself and others.*

~Shantideva, *Way of the Bodhisattva*

A few years ago, the Mississippi River began to flood, threatening to devastate many towns and cities in the American Midwest. One of those was Quincy, Illinois, where residents worked day and night securing vulnerable areas with thousands of sandbags. Fatigue and pessimism began to set in on the residents as they dealt with declining resources and increasing water levels.

Their spirits were uplifted powerfully when they learned that residents of a small city in Massachusetts had taken up a collection and purchased supplies, which were already en route. That kindness came from people who lived in Quincy, Massachusetts.

Based on the fact that the two communities shared the same name, Quincy, the residents in Massachusetts felt a bond with the people of Quincy, Illinois, which compelled them to reach out and help.

This heart-warming incident provides an excellent backdrop for the words of Shantideva, an eighth century Indian Buddhist teacher. In his book, *The Way of the Bodhisattva*, he advised people who wanted to be on a spiritual path to "strive at first to mediate upon the sameness of yourself and others."

This teaches an antidote to an inferiority complex, "I'm not as good as they are," and to a superiority complex, "I'm better than they are." Shantideva stresses the importance of equality. Once this is realized it becomes easier to stand in the shoes of others, to feel their suffering and to respond with compassion. There is great wisdom in the modern proverb: "We're all in the same boat."

DAY **98**

WHEN CURRENT EVENTS BRING YOU DOWN

It is important not to allow ourselves to be put off by the magnitude of others' suffering. The misery of millions is not a cause for pity. Rather it is a cause for compassion.

~Dalai Lama

The shortest biography of the Buddha can be summed up in two sentences. He was born into privilege and wealth. Then, he saw suffering and was transformed by it.

There is an interesting modern parallel to the experience of the Buddha. The *New York Times* recently published an obituary of a man named Gene Estess. He, like the Buddha, was transformed by suffering, which he witnessed in New York City. Here is his story intertwined with that of the Buddha:

The Buddha was born into unearned privilege.

Gene Estess was born on June 1, 1935, into unearned privilege.

The Buddha's father had great wealth and influence.

Gene Estess's father, as the owner of a department store, had great wealth and influence.

The Buddha saw suffering and was transformed.

Gene Estess saw suffering and was transformed.

The Buddha walked away from the family wealth and inheritance

Gene Estess walked away from his family wealth and inheritance.

The Buddha received an excellent education.

Gene Estess attended America's finest universities, graduating from the Wharton School of Business at the University of Pennsylvania.

Gene Estess was a Wall Street financier who prospered greatly in that livelihood. Then, one auspicious evening in 1984, Gene Estess was walking through Grand Central Terminal with hundreds of others. He was catching a train to his beautiful suburban estate in Westchester County.

As he made his way to the train, he saw a woman sitting with a black poodle, among the homeless who made their home inside Grand Central during the 1980s.

That woman and her poodle became etched in Gene Estess's mind, so the next day he introduced himself to her. The woman said her name was Patricia and her poodle was named Ebony. Patricia was soft spoken and had a gentle voice. She liked to write and carried numerous notebooks with disconnected writings, which was common to someone suffering with schizophrenia. That day, Gene Estess gave the woman $5. It was the first of many regular donations he made to the woman, who was addicted, homeless and suffered with mental illness.

Wanting to help her more, Gene Estess discovered the Jericho Project, a Manhattan based nonprofit, and arranged for Patricia and Ebony to reside there.

His encounter with Patricia and Ebony was profound. By 1987, Gene Estess had enough of managing and making money, so he quit his extraordinarily high-paying work and accepted an offer to become the director of Jericho Project. He worked without pay for the first year, and thereafter, earned around $17,000 yearly. His colleagues on Wall Street said he was "nuts" and "crazy" and that he had "lost himself." Gene Estess served as director for eighteen years before retiring in 2005.

The Buddha was a nontheist. He didn't believe in God.

Gene Estess was a nontheist. When asked about his dramatic transformation, he said simply and directly, "Please understand. It was nothing religious. It wasn't god-like."

Here's the lesson from the lives of the Buddha and Gene Estess: the proper response to seeing suffering is not to recoil, not to break down and weep, but to be transformed by it. Both men, upon witnessing suffering, became better human beings as a result of what they saw.

DAY **99**

KNOWING WHEN IT'S TIME TO BREAK UP

It is more difficult to murder a phantom than a reality.

~Virginia Woolf

Once there was a king who had gifted his daughter with a beautiful diamond necklace. Sadly, the necklace was stolen, leaving his daughter heartbroken. The king offered a reward of fifty gold coins to anyone who found it. Word spread rapidly about the sizable reward.

A few days later a man was walking along a polluted river next to an industrial area. Suddenly, he saw something shimmering in the river and when he looked closely, he saw the diamond necklace. Wanting to claim the reward, he put his hand into the polluted river, grabbing at the necklace. Somehow he kept missing it and could not grasp it. Looking again, he saw the necklace was still there.

This time he waded into the river, using both arms to catch the necklace. But, strangely, he still missed the necklace! He came out and sat on the riverbank feeling depressed. Then again he saw the necklace, right there. This time he was determined to get it. He plunged into the dirty river and searched everywhere, and yet he failed.

Just then a sage who was walking by saw him and asked him what was going on. He told the sage about the necklace and how he had tried repeatedly to grab it without success. The sage then told him to try looking upward toward the branches of the tree instead of the polluted river. The man looked up and sure enough, the necklace was dangling from the branch of a tree. He had been trying to capture a mere reflection of the real necklace all that time!

The story is about illusions. Some of the most common illusions we cling to include:

* I'll by happy when . . . (Reality: The ideal time to be happy isn't in the future—it's now, in the present moment.)

* I'll start exercising, start dieting, quit smoking, quit drinking, etc., soon . . . (Reality: Commitments delayed are commitments denied.)

* I'll do that when I have more time . . . (Reality: If something is important to us, we make the time.)

* I'll get there faster if . . . (Reality: We never arrive at a destination until we're ready, so enjoy the journey.)

* I can change him/her . . . (Reality: The only person you can change is yourself.)

* I have control over . . . (Reality: The only control you have is over your mind.)

* I'm a self-made man/woman . . . (Reality: There's been help from others along the way.)

✤ She/he had instant success . . . (Reality: There's no
such thing. All success is based on the foundation of
persistent, persevering hard work.)

To have an authentic and satisfying life you need to have the
proper perspective in order not to live under the power of your
illusions. You need to look where the "diamonds" really are and
not at the illusion on the water.

LONELINESS CAN BE A GOOD THING

We are always up and down. It's not our body that goes up and down, it's our mind. Therefore sometimes we have to examine ourselves.

~Lama Thubten Yeshe

Most people don't know that yoga was instrumental in developing one of the world's first martial arts, called Kalaripayattu. Ancient Buddhist monks would learn martial arts to protect themselves against thieves, and teach martial arts all over Asia. Those who participate in Kalari Payat adhere to the following code of conduct:

1. Discipline.

2. Respect for the teacher.

3. Regularity in practice.

4. Strength in body and in mind.

5. Patience.

6. Humility.

7. Humanity.

8. Respect for tradition.

9. Respect for oneself, and courage.

10. The search for peace.

We human beings have a duty to evolve spiritually and emotionally. Doing that means self-observation in order to experience self-transformation. Carefully read and reflect on the Kalari Payat code of conduct, using it to examine your life, your living. Here's how to conduct this kind of spiritual and emotional audit.

1. Discipline. Am I disciplined in thought, word and deed?

2. Respect for the teacher. Do I respect those who have taught me important life lessons?

3. Regularity in practice. Am I regularly engaged in practices which are important in my life?

4. Strength in body and mind. Am I careful about maintaining a healthy body and mind?

5. Patience. Am I patient with those around me, above me and below me?

6. Humility. Do others see me as modest and gentle?

7. Humanity. Am I humane, that is, kind, gracious, generous?

8. Respect for tradition. Do I appreciate the long lineage of persons who have preserved, protected and promoted the values which are important to me?

9. Respect for oneself, and courage. If I respect myself I will have the courage of my convictions. Is this true about myself?

10. The search for peace. Am I diligent and disciplined about searching for peace and, in its absence, creating the environment for peace to flourish?

DAY **101**

SURVIVING RUSH WEEK

All that we are is the result of what we have thought.
The mind is everything. What we think we become.

~Buddha

All people think.

There are no exceptions.

To think is a universal human trait.

And it is how we think which determines whether we see our lives as positive or negative, blessed or burdened.

From time to time we all hear about a people whose lives have been exceptionally difficult. They've had to deal with one challenge after another, one hardship after another. Yet, they step up to the challenge, deal with what has come their way, and continue to exhibit optimism, hope, even peace and serenity.

We also hear about people whose lives have been exceptionally privileged. They enjoy good health, have ample discretionary money, live in affluent communities. In spite of all that, they are unhappy, restless, unfulfilled, even feeling miserable.

The difference between these two types of people comes down to their thoughts. Though some must overcome great difficulties, they think of themselves as fortunate and are therefore content. Though others enjoy all the comforts of life, they think of themselves as unfortunate and therefore become discontent.

How do you think about your life—blessed or burdened? The answer is all in how you understand it. Author Melvin McLeod wisely observed: "the mind is the source of both our suffering and our joy."

DAY **102**

LESSON FROM A MEDITATING DOG

*I did not begin when I was born, nor when I was
conceived. I have been growing, developing, through
incalculable myriads of millenniums. All my previous
selves have their voices, echoes, promptings in me.*

~Jack London

At a Buddhist center in northern India, a stray dog entered the
meditation hall and sat on one of the meditation cushions. This
made the head monk break into a huge smile. As the monks
chanted in unison, the dog threw back his head and howled with
the monks. It sounded as though the creature howled in tune
with chant.

Two monks gently picked up the creature and carried
him out, only to have him scramble right back in and onto the
cushion. Once again, the dog threw his head back and howled
with the monks.

When it came time for a teaching lesson, the head monk
explained the reason why stray dogs like to hang around
Buddhist temples. They came not merely for the food and the

kind company, but perhaps because the dogs, in a past life, were weak monks and are now seeking to earn their way back to their rightful place.

Reincarnation is an important concept in Eastern thought, but even if you have doubts about it, think about these questions: What are you drawn to? Why are you drawn to it? Where does that interest come from? Some people—even very young ages—are naturally drawn to music, art, sports, spirituality, commerce. Some would say they have an innate aptitude for these things. But did that just begin when they were born or, as Jack London says, is it the result of growing and developing across millenniums?

DAY **103**

SPEAKING UP CONFIDENTLY IN SEMINAR

Not having the confidence of thinking, "I can do it," we end up doing nothing.

~Ringu Tulku Rinpoche

Kuda Bux (1905–1981) was an Indian Yogi and mystic who had incredible control over his mind. One of his astonishing feats was fire walking, something he demonstrated all over the world. In 1935 he visited England, where he demonstrated his fire-walking ability before an audience of scientists from the University of London. A trench was formed, 12 feet long, 6 feet wide and 3 feet deep. Into the trench, 7 tons of oak logs, 1 ton of firewood and 10 gallons of oil were set ablaze and allowed to burn for several hours. The surface temperature was read at 806° F while deeper inside the glowing embers, the heat registered 2,552°F, which is hot enough to melt steel.

Bux walked through the coals unscathed. His feet were checked before and after the fire-walking demonstration to verify that no protective chemicals, topical creams or herbs were used. After Bux walked across the fire once, a photographer who couldn't get his camera to work asked for a retake. Bux obliged and repeated the fire walk. As it was a windy day, papers which drifted across the trench immediately burst into flames. When Bux was asked how he could do the fire walk, he simply explained it as "faith."

What does he mean when he uses the word "faith"? Buddhism does teach that we need to have faith if we are to advance and evolve spiritually. However, Buddhists don't use the word faith to mean rigid and uncritical acceptance of dogma. When the word "faith" shows up in Buddhist thinking, it means confidence. Perhaps Kuda Bux's response to the question, "How did you do that?" could simply have been the word "confidence." He had faith or confidence in his teachings about mind control; he had faith or confidence in his teachers who taught him to control his mind; and ultimately, he had faith or confidence in himself. As a result he was able to overcome his "problem"— the fire and heat.

Use the example of Kuda Bux to assess your own self-confidence level. Do you believe in yourself? If not, why not? And, if not, why not change that way of thinking? You are not trapped or imprisoned into that way of thinking. It's just a habit and habits can be broken.

DAY **104**

GOING FOR A 4.0 GPA

*The potential of the human mind is subject to and limited
only by our individual beliefs or unbelief as to whether
we can accomplish a thing or not. Human mind power
is evidenced in the fact that we always get to be right.*

~Chuck Danes

Many centuries ago in India, a village was terrorized by a tiger
who was clearly infected with rabies. One of the village elders
ventured into the woods at night armed with bow and arrow. The
elder was not a particularly talented archer but he was better
than most in the village. While hidden behind some bushes, he
saw a figure resembling the tiger in the distance, so he pulled
back on the bow with all his might and released the arrow.

Uncertain whether or not the animal was dead, he waited
until sunlight before venturing out to examine the animal. To his
amazement, he discovered that his arrow was deeply embedded
in a large rock. He was intrigued that he could release an arrow
and have it penetrate a solid rock so he walked back several
yards to attempt to repeat this feat. Each arrow that he released
bounced off the rock, barely leaving a scratch. This baffled him.

Finally, it dawned on him that during the night, when he could not see clearly and assumed the rock was the tiger, that he believed the object was penetrable. And so it was. However, during the day, when he saw the rock as a rock, he no longer had the power to have the arrow penetrate the rock.

In ancient India, archers were trained not only in how to use the bow and arrow but they spent hours in deep meditation training the mind. Records from that time indicate that master archers could direct their arrows by the power of the mind, accurately striking targets hundreds of yards away and penetrating hard objects.

The common thread between the village elder and ancient Indian archers is the way they used their mind. They had the belief that, without a doubt, they could strike and penetrate the target. When the mind is focused this way, it becomes a "super" mind.

So, what is the impenetrable obstacle holding you back in your life? Why not begin to cultivate faith in yourself, in your abilities, in the powers of your mind to penetrate and overcome that obstacle? President Franklin Delano Roosevelt wisely noted, "Men and women are not prisoners of fate, but only prisoners of their own minds."

DAY **105**

BUDDHIST WISDOM VIA GREEK PHILOSOPHY

Nearly all the philosophical and mathematical doctrines attributed to Pythagoras are derived from India.

~Ludwig von Schroder

There is ample archaeological and philological evidence that ancient Indian spiritual philosophies were well-known and highly respected in Greece. In particular, many of the most famous Greek philosophers sound very Buddhist. In fact, the Buddha was teaching around the same time that Greek philosophy was at its peak. Consider these bits of wisdom from five Greek philosophers.

Pythagoras (c. 570–c. 495 BCE)

On the importance of inner work:

Some are slaves to money or ambition but others are interested in understanding life itself...and they value the contemplation and discovery of nature beyond all other pursuits.

On vegetarianism:

*As long as man continues to be the ruthless destroyer of
lower living beings he will never know health or peace.
For as long as men massacre animals, they will kill each
other.*

On observing our thoughts and managing them:

A thought is an idea in transit.

Heraclitus (c. 535–c. 475 BCE)

On being careful about what we put into our minds:

*Day by day, what you choose, what you think and what
you do is who you become.*

On the impermanence of life:

*Everything flows and nothing abides, everything gives
way and nothing stays fixed. Also this statement: No man
ever steps in the same river twice, for it's not the same
river and he's not the same man.*

Socrates (c. 469–c. 399 BCE)

On having a Zen "don't know mind":

The only true wisdom is knowing you know nothing.

On the dangers of an overactive life:

Beware the bareness of a busy life.

Aristotle (c. 384–c. 322 BCE)

On moving from head to heart:

*Educating the mind without educating the heart is no
education at all.*

On mind management:

*It is the mark of an educated man to be able to entertain
a thought without accepting it.*

Democritus (c. 460–c. 370 BCE)

On karma:

Everywhere man blames nature and fate, yet his fate is mostly but the echo of his character and passion, his mistakes and his weaknesses.

On intention and motive:

Good means not merely not to do wrong, but rather not to desire to do wrong.

On happiness as an "inside job":

Happiness resides not in possessions and not in gold; happiness dwells in the soul.

DAY **106**

TACKLING TOUGH COURSES

You gain strength, courage, and confidence by every experience in which you really stop to look fear in the face. You must do the thing which you think you cannot do.

~Eleanor Roosevelt

Tibetan spiritual teacher Chogyam Trungpa was the guest at a fourth grade class, where he talked about his life in Tibet and about escaping from the Chinese Communists into India. During the question time, one boy asked Trungpa if he was ever afraid. Trungpa explained that part of his Buddhist training included spending time in "scary places" such as graveyards. The purpose of these types of experiences, he explained, was to learn there is often nothing to be afraid of. Then, he told the class about a time he was traveling with companions to a Buddhist monastery. As they neared the gates, he saw a large dog. Though it was chained, the creature barked loudly, bared it fangs and displayed aggressive red eyes. Keeping their eyes on the dog but also maintaining distance, the group carefully made their way to the gate.

Suddenly, the chain broke and the dog ran at them. Several of the members began to run as quickly as they could for safety while others froze in fear. Trungpa, however, turned and ran as fast as he could *toward the dog*! This unnerved the dog who put his tail between his legs and ran off. Based on that experience and others, Trungpa often taught that it was important to lean into the sharp points of life.

An important life lesson is this: when we face something which frightens us there are times when we should face it rather than flee from it. Some effective ways of learning to deal with fears include:

- ❀ Leaning into things which frighten you. When you fear something move toward it rather than way from it. This simple act strengthens resolve and builds courage.

- ❀ Practicing positive thinking regularly so that your dominant thoughts are optimistic and hopeful not negative and fearful.

- ❀ Replacing fear thoughts with ones which focus on ways that you are innovative, creative, and solution oriented.

- ❀ Recalling past successes. Think back to times when you dealt with something which was initially frightening but you stepped up to the challenge and were successful.

Chevalier performed publicly and perfectly. He would remember his doctor's words on many future occasions when he experienced doubts and moments of fear. Chevalier's action reveals the wisdom of Ralph Waldo Emerson's insight: "Do the thing you fear and the death of fear is certain." Face your fears directly and they become downsized.

THE FOUR-YEAR GRADUATION PLAN

Just as a rock of one solid mass remains unshaken
by the wind, even so neither visible forms, nor sounds,
no scents, nor tastes nor bodily impressions, neither
the desired nor the undesired, can cause such a one to
waver. Steadfast is his mind, gained is deliverance.

~Pali Canon

A monk was out begging from house to house in a village. One door was opened by a beautiful woman who was the wife of a wealthy villager. She decided to see if the monk could be tempted to break any of his vows, so she invited him into her home under the pretense of being a spiritual seeker. There she engaged him in conversation. After some time had passed, the monk said he needed to be on his way, excused himself and went to the door, discovering it was locked.

"Please open the door," he asked the woman.

"Not just yet," was her response. "I will let you out of this room only if you do one of the following: kill the goat who is tied up outside the back door; have sex with me; or drink this jug of wine."

He was in a dilemma. As a Buddhist he could not resort to violence by fighting with the woman to get out of her house. Furthermore, her three conditions all violated the vows he took to become a Buddhist monk. Slaughtering the goat would mean breaking the precept against killing. Having sex would be breaking his vow of celibacy. Drinking from the jug would violate the precept of avoiding intoxicating drinks. Eventually, the troubled monk decided that the least offensive thing he could do would be to drink the wine, which would harm no one but himself.

Because he wasn't used to drinking liquor of any kind, the monk got drunk. Because he was drunk, his resolve was weakened and he became mindless and careless. Furthermore, the liquor made him hungry, so he killed the goat. While it was cooking, he had sex with the woman.

This story is well-known in Buddhist circles, where it is often referred to as the Tale of the Hapless Monk. It is a reminder to us that our commitments, promises and vows are interlinked. Compromising in one area can create a domino effect where we find ourselves sliding deeper and deeper in a quagmire. When obstacles or temptations present themselves, just say, "No, I will not allow this to derail my commitment." Choose to be like a rock, a solid mass that remains "unshaken by the wind."

DAY **108**

BODY BUILDING

*To keep the body in good health is a duty, otherwise we
shall not be able to keep ourselves mind strong and clear.*

~Buddha

The Buddha taught that the body is very important; that it is
vital to keep the body healthy and strong. A healthy body offers
two advantages over an unhealthy one. First, a vigorous body
strengthens the mind, intensifying your ability for spiritual growth
and evolution. Second, a strong body can be used to help other
beings whereas an unhealthy, sick one is limited. Here are three
Buddhist "P"s—guidelines for maintaining a healthy body.

1. Proper eating. The Buddha promoted balance and
   cautioned against indulgence and abuse of the body.
   Eating the right amount versus eating too much or too
   little is the objective. Meat eating is discouraged or should
   be limited in favor of fresh fruits, vegetable, and grains.

2. Proper rest. This can be a struggle for college students
   dealing with academic requirements—reading,
   researching, writing, studying, taking exams. Precisely
   because of those stresses, it's vital to focus on getting the

right amount of sleep for your body. Again, balance is the key. Too much or too little sleep are to be avoided.

3. Proper exercise. Physical activity keeps the body strong, healthy and supple while reducing stress at the same time. Find an exercise which works for your temperament—jogging, walking, biking, swimming, weight lifting, dancing, yoga, pilates, etc.—and then do it several times a week.

As you go through a busy semester—classes, homework, studying, meetings, maintaining your social life—don't neglect or take your body for granted. Give it the respect it deserves.

ABOUT THE AUTHOR

Victor M. Parachin, M. Div., is director of the Tulsa Yoga Meditation Center and the author of several books about yoga, meditation and Eastern spiritual practices.